GASCONY AND THE PYRENEES:
ENGLAND'S FIRST EMPIRE

JOHN EAST

GASCONY AND THE PYRENEES

ENGLAND'S FIRST EMPIRE

★

JOHNSON

LONDON

First Published 1970

ISBN 0 85307 087 3

SET IN 11 ON 12 POINT BASKERVILLE, PRINTED AND MADE IN GREAT BRITAIN
BY CLARKE, DOBLE AND BRENDON LTD., PLYMOUTH
JOHNSON PUBLICATIONS LTD., 11/14 STANHOPE MEWS WEST, LONDON, S.W. 7

CONTENTS

A BOOK FOR BARBARA

INTRODUCTION

The South West corner of France, the wide sweep of the Atlantic coast running south from Bordeaux to the country of the Basques and eastwards up into the high peaks of the Pyrenees themselves, is an area that will be always associated with England and the English. Indeed for many years it was a part of England and was ruled by the English crown, and it was here that they have come as soldiers, traders and travellers. Today we can still find remains of these associations and retrace the footsteps of those who went before.

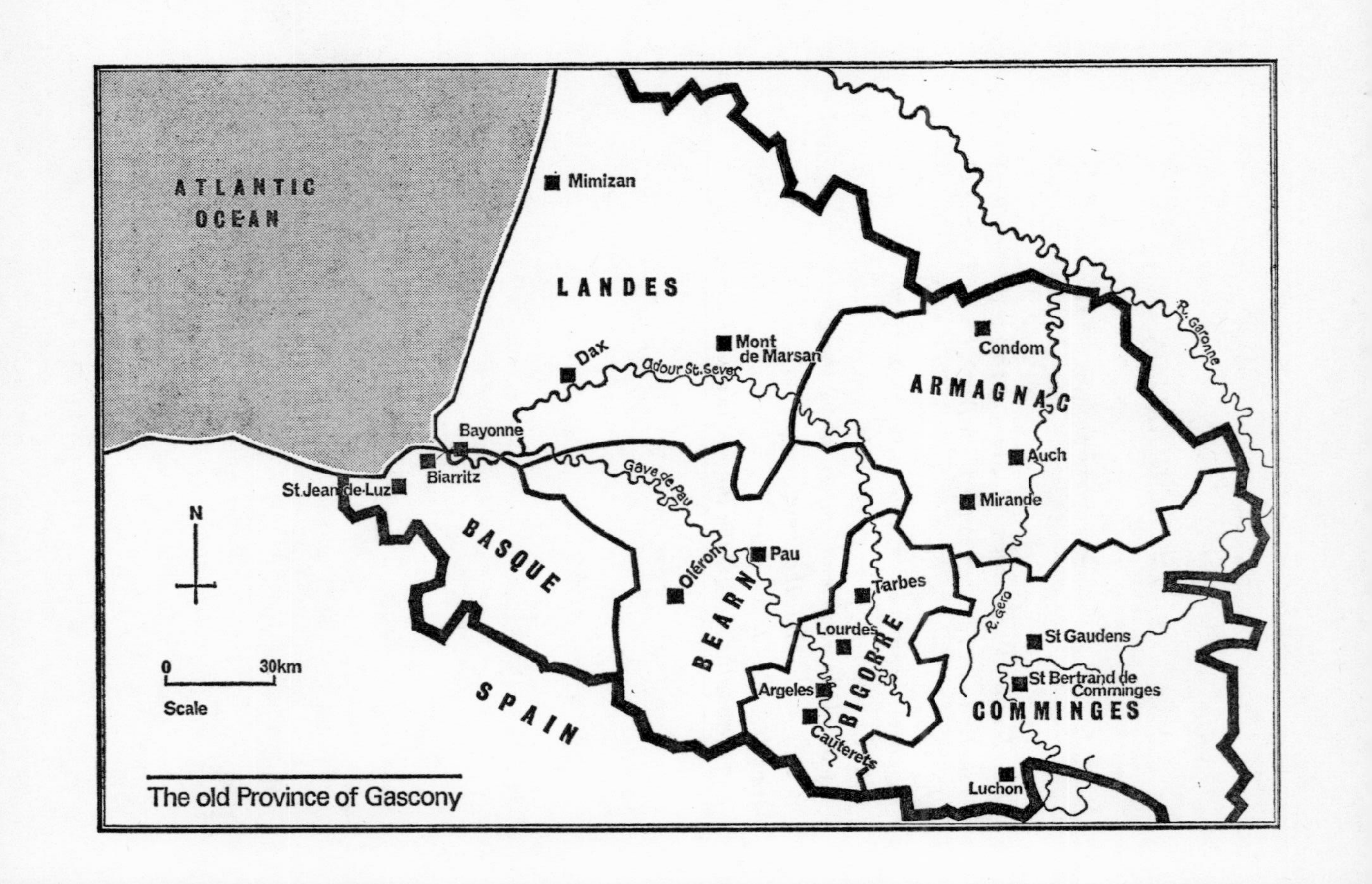

The old Province of Gascony

I

A REGION OF HISTORY

THE very name of Gascony still has a ring in English ears. It conjures up images of the gallant knights of the orders of chivalry of the Middle Ages, when the Gascons themselves lived under English rule and fought alongside the English in their battles with the French. For three hundred years the English were here and the names of the great towns and fortresses like Dax, Mont de Marsan or Bayonne were as well known in England as many places in our own island.

Later when the English were finally forced from their last strongholds, it was only a short time before they returned to renew the well-established trading links, for here were the fine wines so much enjoyed by the English at a time when the common people drank great tankards of ale while their lords sipped the wines of France. Few drank the water, though this was a habit that was certainly valid in the cities. Bad water is supposed to have killed at least one King of England and certainly one Prince, the Black Prince himself. The great trade in wine continues to this day, although the wines of Gascony never really recovered from the disaster that the phyliloxera scourge brought to it at the end of the nineteenth century. Its near neighbour to the north, the vineyards of Bordeaux, however, kept the English market supplied.

When the troops of Wellington's Peninsular Army passed here in 1814, in many areas they were greeted almost as liberators by the local people. It is said that if you see a fair haired blue eyed child playing in one of the small villages, it is a living proof that English soldiers came that way.

But this region is known to us in other ways. Travel for pleasure is a new idea and only a consequence of improved communications rather than the cause. One of the first regions to be visited in this way was the South West of France. Its fine resorts came into prominence at about the same time as the resorts of the Côte d'Azur, which also owe their origins to the first travelling Britons. In literature too, Gascony and the Gascons always have a rather larger than life role to play. Who has not thrilled to the adventures of D'Artagnan and his musketeers?

Napoleon in one of his bursts of administrative energy laid out a system of dividing France into small local administrative units known as Departments. Over each department he set up a representative of his own central authority, the Prefect. These departments replaced the old provinces of France at one fell stroke of the pen. But the old provinces did not die, one cannot even say they faded away, and Gascony itself remained a very real entity. It is a region dominated by great natural features, on one side the sea, the distant stretches of the Atlantic almost pulling the people to sail away to remote lands to new adventures. To the south looming over the whole land is the bulky mass of the Pyrenees, a compact but spiky ridge of mountains. Here it is said Africa begins, and even today in high summer one can see that symbol of Africa, the grotesque vulture gliding and wheeling over the mountain tops, keeping itself aloft apparently by gently waving its wing tips. Few valleys cut into the mountains themselves which run steeply to the plains. To the north a more arbitrary boundary is drawn separating it from the ancient Duchy of Garonne. From the coast just south of Mimizan the line runs east, passing just to the north of Condom, then north almost to the old city of Agen, then south passing well to the west of Toulouse skirting the old Comté of Foix to reach the Pyrenees at St Girons.

Within this wide ranging region are naturally and to some extent less naturally many subdivisions. Perhaps the most important of these is the Basque country, the Eskual Herri, the land of those who speak the Eskuara or Basque language. Its limits are not easy to define for it is rather a frontier of language than of political systems. In practice it covers roughly an area running south from Bayonne on the Adour river, along the coast into Spain as far as Bilbao. Inland the limits are less easy to define but of the seven Basque provinces three are in France, Labourd, Basse Navarre and Soule, all within the department of the Basses Pyrenees; while four are in Spain, Guipuzcoa, Biscaye on the coast, and Navarre and Alava inland.

Immediately adjacent to this unique land of the Basques is the Béarn, one of the oldest names in France. Its fiercely independent people maintained all their old privileges and rights long after they were incorporated into the French state in 1620.

Thus Gascony is dominated by sea and mountain. Its rivers run down from the Pyrenees to the sea or joining together make up the waterways that flood down to the Adour or the Garonne.

The Pyrenees are a great mountain massif, made up of part granite and part sedimentary rock formations. This has led to the strange skylines of steep rocky peaks, while nearby are more softly-rounded slopes and plateaux. The high peaks of the range rise up to 10,000 feet with the Pic du Midi 9,500 feet, the Neouvielle 10,150 feet, the Vignemale 10,800 feet and the Balaitous 10,300 feet. The central Pyrenees were swept by great glaciers in the time of the ice ages and have left us today with the awe-inspiring Cirques cut out of the older mountain blocks. The most famous of these are Gavarnie and Troumouse. The valleys that lead into the mountains are few and narrow and communication between them is difficult. Often it is simpler to redescend to the plain to reach another valley rather than cross the mountains. These valleys are the natural waterways and the swift flowing streams, variously known as Gaves, Nestes or Nives, rush down to provide the energy for the hydro-electricity stations, the water needed on the plains below and, of course, the famous fishing, particularly trout.

At the western end of the mountains in the Basque area the slopes are less abrupt and the countryside is typified by broad valleys and low-sweeping hills. This region is already fertile to a degree unknown but a short distance away in the mountains. Further north is the plain of the Landes. Here remain wide stretches of sand. Its origin is undoubtedly from the seashore and it was transported inland by the strong Atlantic gales. The sand has been fixed in place by careful afforestation with pines, started as far back as the eighteenth century. This has enabled the population, who previously had eked out a frugal living by fishing from a few small coastal villages, to move inland and recommence the now flourishing agriculture.

Agriculture is in fact the foremost activity of Gascony. Under a sky, gay and varied, as one French geographer quaintly put it, many crops and animals grow and flourish. Great fields of maize, brought back by the Basques from South America, wheat, the vines of the Armagnac, all stretch across the region. Flocks of sheep wander amongst the pines of the Landes to the slopes of the High Pyrenees, where cattle still travel with their herdsmen on the annual movement, the transhumance. One of the few places where the vast movement of animals and their keepers takes place every spring, from the lower valleys to the very edge of the bare rock of the mountain peaks, and the return, just before the first winter snows come towards the end of September, still exists.

On the plains of Béarn, in the Landes and further north in the Armagnac is one of the best known of France's poultry raising areas. Chickens, ducks and perhaps most important geese are bred in large numbers, and are the basic necessities for the excellent local dishes.

But what of the Gascons themselves? Despite the rapid development of communications, new roads, railways and air travel, life for most people outside the main towns is a solitary affair. Villages are small and scattered and in the mountains for the long winter months travel is not easy even today. The people have a reputation for being good businessmen but also very prudent. Often they have emigrated, particularly to South America, but they always return to pass their declining years in their home district. This is also part of their traditional love of adventure which dates back to the Gascons who rode with Joan of Arc or in more modern times to those who fought with success against the Germans in the Resistance. They have remained straightforward and loyal, outspoken but courteous, hospitable but formal.

How is it then that these people have kept an identifiable separate way of life? The first recorded inhabitants were the Iberians who swept down from the Pyrenees as far north as the Garonne river. Here they clashed with the Celtic tribes who held the land to the far bank. This rivalry continued until the coming of the Romans in 56 B.C. The Iberians were an intelligent and industrious people, but quickly overrun by the all powerful Roman legions of Crassus, they soon submitted and adopted the customs and even the language of their conquerors. But with the collapse of Rome under the attacks of the Barbarian hordes life changed rapidly, and the whole region was divided and subdivided, pillaged, depopulated, time and again. However, around the end of the sixth century A.D.

power was gradually taken into the hands of a Pyrenean tribe, the Vascons. So the land of the western Pyrenees became known as Vasconie, but was little different from the Gascony of today.

The eighth century brought yet another threat, the invasion of the Moors from across the Pyrenees. The Moslem peoples, masters of North Africa and most of Spain were thrusting north into Europe in what seemed an unstoppable flood.

The great leader, Charles Martel, was to save Europe and Christianity itself at the battle of Poitiers. The Moors fled back south across the mountains destroying everything in their path. The Vascons inevitably now moved under the rule of Charles Martel and the Holy Roman Empire of Charlemagne. But frequent revolts against the imperial power were harshly crushed. After the death of Charlemagne in 814 troubles again pressed hard. This time in the form of the dreaded Viking ships. From 844 onwards every spring saw the long low warships sweep up the estuaries and rivers of the west coast of France. One after another the towns were attacked and destroyed. Dax, Tarbes, Bayonne, Condom all fell. Not until the tenth century when the Northmen settled in Normandy did any stable form of government or even organised life resume. Now local rulers, the Dukes of Gascony, emerged and, although divided, the region still remained outside the power of the new kings of France. Religion became a great power in the land. Churches and monasteries were built, the towns destroyed by the Vikings were rebuilt. This was in large measure due to the vast movement of peoples of the Middle Ages, the pilgrimages; and the greatest pilgrimage of all was to the tomb of St James at Compostella just south of the Pyrenees on the Spanish coast of Galicia. Five of the great routes to Compostella ran through Gascony and all along their way were built the hospitals, the religious houses where the pilgrims could find shelter.

In 1137 a man died in Compostella, an event which was

perhaps the single most important event in the history of Gascony, for the man was William VIII, Duke of Aquitaine. He had only just married his daughter Eleanor to Louis the heir to the throne of France. As the old Salic law did not apply in Aquitaine she became the sole ruler of the whole province, of which Gascony was a part. Soon her husband became King, but all was not well. King Louis was religious, serious, reserved whilst his wife was fun loving, wilful and a personality to be reckoned with. After ten years of marriage they were divorced in 1152.

Soon afterwards she married the young Prince Henry Plantagenet, who, within two years was to become King of England and master of one third of the territory of France. Thus in a few short months the Gascons passed under the Kings of France and from them to England, where they were to remain for three hundred years.

For many years the Gascons struggled against this alien rule and even called on the kings of France to aid them. When Philip VI came to the throne of France in 1328 he listened to these pleas and started a series of armed interventions which led soon to the interminable struggle of the Hundred Years War. The armies of the English were now to come and fight; and stay and rule. Here, too, was the base for the great raids into France of the Black Prince. For many years the tide of fortune swept against the French; the English devastated their homelands, their king was captured and taken to London where he was held against a vast ransom; their great knight Du Guesclin was also captured and held by the Black Prince; and after their defeats bands of French and English soldiers, the so-called Free Companies, looted and destroyed right across the frontier areas of Gascony. Towards the end of the fourteenth century, with the deaths of the Black Prince, his father Edward III, Charles V and Du Guesclin the war began to lose in ferocity. England and France were both ruled by children, Charles VI of France who was twelve years old and

Richard II of England who was ten. However with the turn of the century the French began to gather strength with the great crusade of Joan of Arc. The Gascon lords at last supported the King of France in a national campaign to reunite their country. Hostilities commenced in 1438 and by 1451 virtually all of Aquitaine had been retaken by the French. The next year Talbot lead an English revival, but when he was killed at Castillon it was the end of the English cause in South West France. Gascony was finally linked to the French crown.

But peace was still not to come to this corner of France; over the next hundred years religion was to be the cause of great strife and a whole series of campaigns, as first one faction then another forced their claims. Eventually King Louis XIII occupied Gascony once again for the crown in 1620. Immediately afterwards Cardinal Richelieu commenced his campaign to pacify France. One of his most effective methods was the removal of the fortifications that had been built up to such strength during the turbulent times of the Middle Ages. Town walls were levelled, strongholds and castles were smashed down. Today, although still rich in architectural treasures, Gascony has only here and there a fortification or old wall to mark its militant history.

Now central power was firmly in the hands of the Kings of France and here it was to remain until the Revolution in 1789. Although still racked with religious dissent during this period Gascony at last began to prosper. In one hundred years population increased by one hundred and fifty per cent, china and porcelain industries were developed, agriculture prospered, the thermal waters of the Pyrenees were exploited.

The Revolution served only to increase the central power established in Paris and the region suffered once again, churches and Christianity were banned, the young men called to serve in the new armies. Many conscripts never reached their regiments and fled into the mountains or over the frontier into Spain. Many formed themselves into marauding bands attacking travellers and even besieging castles. This state of affairs was to last until 1815.

It was to Gascony that British troops first came in 1813 after their long campaign in Spain forcing their way over the passes of the Pyrenees and at last into France itself in pursuit of the army of Marshall Soult. In later years political stability brought commercial prosperity in its wake until the end of the nineteenth century when agriculture, the main source of wealth, began to decline and despite the increase in demand during the first World War there has been a gradual movement from the land ever since. Now, however, as we shall see new industries and new techniques are coming to play their part in the life of the Gascons.

II

THE LANDES

TRAVELLING south from Bordeaux one soon reaches the long flat coastal plain of the Landes, running due south for one hundred and fifty miles. The vast sandy beach grows at the rate of a thousand cubic yards of sand every year, gradually building up and then blowing inland. For much of its early history this region was literally a desert, inhospitable, bleak, virtually unable to support the most meagre existence.

Man has always known that moving sand can be halted by planting of strong vegetation or trees, but so strong was the movement of the sand that all attempts to hold it in check failed, until an engineer named Bremontier managed to solve the problem by complicated use of walls made from stakes, which made rough sea walls from the dunes themselves. These were fixed in place by fast growing grasses. The great dunes on the inland side were then tackled in their turn with shrubs and pines. The shrubs growing up first to shelter the slower-developing pines.

By the mid-nineteenth century the main difficulties posed by the sand had been overcome but yet another threat remained, the land on the interior of the sand belt had a layer of impervious rock some few inches below the surface, so that for most of the winter months the whole area was nothing more than a huge bog. The rock or *alios* was finally broken up by engineers under the direction of Chambrelent who extended the forests on the coastal strip adding cork oaks and evergreen trees. The whole region now began to prosper and the prosperity was based on the forests. Wood was produced in great quantities, pit props for the mines of the north and across the sea to England, resins were tapped for glue, paper and cork were manufactured while sheep grazed the tough grass on the dunes themselves. In recent years however the forests have suffered badly from fires, particularly during the frequent hot dry summers. Much has been done to minimise the risks of fire, but once it starts a forest fire is one of the most difficult phenomena to halt and usually many thousands of acres are destroyed.

On the southern edge of the forest area is a rich agricultural zone where poultry are produced in large numbers, and it is to this, that the area has turned to base its reputation for fine food, the local specialities include the famous preserved goose or duck and *foie gras*.

Along the coast are many small seaside resorts of the so called Côte d'Argent; in all cases they have a superb beach washed by the powerful Atlantic rollers. Perhaps the largest of these is Mimizan, once a port of some importance; it was silted up by the ever moving sand, which later covered the old town itself. Nearby is the old abbey church which was saved from the encroaching sand by experimental planting of grasses. The huge square bell tower was once used as a lighthouse. Inside there is a romanesque doorway dating from the twelfth century with an interesting tympanum. Mimizan Plage stands some miles from the present town of Mimizan. This pleasant resort is divided into two by the Courant which flows down from an *étang* or inland lake, one of the many such lakes that are often the remains of old watercourses cut off by the sand. It was at Mimizan Plage that the first French fliers to cross the Atlantic from America landed at 1929 and a monument overlooks their landing place from a high dune.

Standing a short distance inland and to the south is the small town of Léon, in the pleasant town square are some interesting old houses built in the regional style. The *étang* or lake of Léon is surrounded by rich vegetation and the Courant d'Houchet which carries away the surplus water from the lake flows through enchanting woods and fields. It is possible to make the excursion by boat from the lake and it covers some five miles as far as the Bains d'Houchet. The first part of the trip is through a strange green setting, the trees reaching overhead so far that they almost touch. Flowering shrubs abound and at some times of the year, such as August, flowering hibiscus can be seen.

Further south are the twin resorts of Hossegor and Cap Breton. Again they are built around a series of inland lakes. Once Hossegor, too, was a port and the river Adour flowed out to the sea here through what is now a salt-water lake. In the fourteenth century a storm blocked its channel and it found another through Port d'Albret. The sailors from Cap Breton are reputed to have been adventurers and explorers and to have given the name of their home port to the island of Cap Breton at the mouth of the St Lawrence river in Canada long before Christopher Columbus discovered America.

A short distance inland from Hossegor is one of the most important towns of the whole region, Dax. The Romans, those experts in thermal baths and health giving springs, soon discovered the possibilities offered by the waters. It took them several years before they could settle here, for there was strong local resistance. However, once established, the Romans brought prosperity and visitors came to seek the cure they hoped the waters offered. They still come to this day. Little remains of its history, the old town walls dating back to the Romans were removed in recent times, despite many local protests. Under English rule Dax maintained its popularity, while its importance as a route centre made it one of the towns always strongly held by English troops.

The cathedral is a vast building on the classical style, built on the site of a Gothic church which collapsed apparently under its own weight. This had in turn replaced an earlier Romanesque church which was reputed to have been built to replace a Merovingian structure. The present cathedral looks firm enough.

Nearby is the more modern church of St Vincent de Xaintes. Here too an earlier series of buildings have been destroyed, but a Gallo-Roman mosaic can still be seen. This was discovered in the foundations of the original church and is possibly the remnants of a temple of Lucinia the goddess of human fertility.

In the centre of the town is the Fontaine Chaude, the hot water fountain, whence the waters pour at a temperature of 147 degrees. The waters are fed from a large tank to various thermal establishments where they are used to treat rheumatic conditions. There is a wide selection of these establishments some being extremely modern and well equipped with swimming pools and mud baths. Dax, too, has a natural beauty all of its own, the river Adour flows quietly and with appropriate dignity between its banks, now made into a park.

Just a few miles to the south is Peyrehorade at the confluence of the Gaves of Pau and Oloron. Just outside the town on a small hill are the remains of the Château d'Aspremont and its great keep. The castle, the property of the Viscomte Orthez was built in 1010, sacked in 1247, rebuilt but burnt down in 1567 by Montgomery, the Protestant General, in the wars of religion. By the bridge across the Gave is the Château de Montreal, also known as the castle of Orthez dating from the sixteenth century.

The main town of the Landes is Mont de Marsan, a centre

of all the roads of the region. Originally it was just a strong-point built by the Emperor Charlemagne in 788 when he was trying to hold the Gascons in subjection, after the slaughter of the rearguard of his army under Roland at Roncevalles. Besieged by Vikings in 841 the town was destroyed several times before being rebuilt in 1141. Here too the English came in the Hundred Years War using the roads that led to the rich areas of France to the east for their great raids. Now Mont de Marsan is an undistinguished country town although it does have a large military training encampment.

One of the main points of attraction is the Arena, where often in the summer months bull fights are held, with the famous matadors coming north from their usual haunts in Spain. But more frequently the Arena is used for the local Course Landaise, which must be one of the most exciting yet picturesque sports in the world. It also has the advantage that the bull is not killed at the end of the bout. There are a number of variations but generally a cow is used and very athletic and dangerous looking cows they are. The cow is held on a long rope and is allowed to charge her opponent, the *écarteur*, who has to use his own agility to dodge and avoid her dashes. He must, however, remain as near as possible without actually being hit by the cow. Often the horns are covered to give extra security. Another event is when the cow is let loose with a cockade attached to her horns and this has to be snatched by fast-running youths.

About a mile outside Mont-de-Marsan is the dramatic new church of St Vincent-de-Paul, built somewhat in the style of the old farmhouses of the Landes, the vast slate roof reaches almost down to the ground.

The Landes today are showing change, no longer can one find the traditional shepherd of the coastal dunes, moving rapidly over the coarse grass on his high stilts, wrapped in his sheepskin coat against the cold Atlantic winds. Perhaps their tradition can still be found in the old shepherd who will show you how he can stand on his stilts and explain some of their folk tales. But now the coast is changing its face again. Petrol has been discovered in the Parentis lake and all the equipment of modern oil drilling now rises above the water.

The southern limit of the Landes is marked by the river Adour running south and then east from Dax growing wider and fuller all the time. Sitting astride this great river where it joins the Nive is the city and port of Bayonne, traditionally the gateway to the country of the Basques.

III

THE MYSTERIOUS PEOPLE

THE Basques are friendly, hardworking but independent people. They speak their own language, the Eskuara, but where they and their language come from is a mystery. The people and the language remain inside the provinces which have been their home since the Middle Ages. How did they come to inhabit this pleasant land where the mountains reach the sea?

It has been suggested that they might have come from virtually any part of Europe you may care to name. One writer, Aymeri Picaud, who prepared notes for pilgrims on the lands through which they had to travel, tells us that in the twelfth century it was thought that the Basques were in fact Scotsmen transported into Spain by Julius Caesar.

The truth of the matter may never be known, for how should this strange language appear at the western extremity of Europe surrounded by tongues all closely linked to Latin. It is evident that the Basques were an itinerant people who brought their language with them possibly from some Asian root. Much work has been done to try to establish some link. Their traditions and history has been studied, their words and speech analysed, their physical features studied but all to little avail.

The first facts that we can discover about the Basques date back to pre-Roman times, when the people inhabiting the western end of the Pyrenees were known for their attacks on travellers and general lawless outlook. The Roman invasion did not meet any great resistance in this area apart from some isolated battles. But it would appear that the Romans did not occupy the territory of the Basques in any permanent fashion, preferring the more fertile plains to the mountain regions. After the fall of Rome the Basques began to expand their lands to cover roughly the present boundaries, and in some places well beyond. Until this time these people had been known as Vascons, but now a difference emerged between the Gascons who lived mostly on the plains or further inland and the Basques themselves grouped around the Atlantic end of the Pyrenees. When Aquitaine passed under English rule the Basques again were left to a large extent to run their own affairs. The Basque provinces in Spain however came under the rule of Navarre and later Castile, although with their *fueros* or ancient rights protected.

Despite the wars that ravaged part of their homeland in the fifteenth century when the French and Spanish struggled long and bitterly, the Basques have been able to maintain their own integrity.

Bayonne, as we have seen, is not truly a Basque town, although many of its inhabitants are undoubtedly Basque. The port has always been important and was fortified by the Romans, but it was under the English that Bayonne came to its full glory. The main port of access to their territories in South West France, it was granted many privileges and advantages by the English. Here came the barrels full of wine to ship to England, oil and leather from Spain, wool from the Landes, while imports included cloth and metals. The needs of the knights helped develop the trade of the armourers and Bayonne became famous for the armour produced there.

The power of the Bayonnais became more and more oppressive, they alone had the right to trade on the sea and to tax supplies for the surrounding areas. This was the start of a feud between the Basques and the people of Bayonne, under their infamous mayor a certain Pé de Puyanne. Pé de Puyanne had been a great sailor in his time and fought with the ships from Bayonne for the English in a number of sea battles, including the decisive clash at Sluys, which broke the power of the French at sea. Here he served well and was reputed to have hung seventy prisoners from his yardarms. As a reward for his services King Edward III appointed him mayor of his native city. He, being a strong man, both physically and in ambitions, began to oppress the Basque communities just outside the city. Cider the staple drink of the Basques was liable to a tax when moved through Bayonne; often the Basques, usually adept at smuggling, avoided this tax. Repressive measures failed to end this abuse even the cutting off of the right hand of any Basque caught smuggling. Eventually outraged by this continued refusal to pay the taxes, and feeling that the Basques had to be taught a lesson, he collected a group of his sailors and on the night of St Bartholomew in 1343 he attacked a party of Basque gentlemen who were peacefully celebrating at the Château of Moitz near the city. Surprised in the castle, many were killed but five were taken prisoner back to Bayonne. Here they were tied to the arches of the bridge so that in the words of the mayor they could find out for themselves that Bayonne had the right to impose taxes as it was a sea port. As the tide rose so the men all drowned and their bodies were left hanging as a reminder of this fact.

Although guards were set at the tower protecting the bridge that night, they did not expect an early vengeance by the Basques, but two hundred Basques under a certain Jean Amacho, a famous Pyrenean hunter suddenly assaulted the tower. Forcing the upper defences they began to descend into the main hall, and here developed a bloody contest, the Battle of the Staircase. It was only when some of the Basques leapt into the hall outflanking the defenders on the stairs that victory was at last secured and all the Bayonnais slaughtered. But in the fight Amacho himself had died. The Basques then removed the bodies of the men drowned at the bridge.

This continued strife could not be allowed to continue so the Black Prince, who held Aquitaine for the King, instructed Lord d'Albret, who represented him in the south, to adjudicate. He ruled, that the people of Bayonne were to blame. The city was heavily fined and the tax on cider removed. In addition he ordered them to build ten churches so that masses could be said for the men drowned at the bridge. Pé de Puyanne was expelled from Bayonne and fled to the protection of the Black Prince at Bordeaux. But Basque vengeance had a long arm, for here he was murdered whilst visiting his own vineyard some two years later.

But Bayonne had other troubles to face, the river Adour which normally flowed into the sea at Cap Breton suddenly changed course in 1310 after a great storm blocked the channel with sand. The river flowed round the obstacle to find a way to the open sea some ten miles further north at Port d'Albret. The new channel was wide, shallow and variable, so that ships began to unload at the river mouth instead of continuing up to the main port. Bit by bit Bayonne started to die. Many attempts were made to open up the old course of the Adour but all without success. It was not until the 1570s a famous engineer, Louis de Foix, persuaded the King to finance an attempt to try once again, that hope revived. For six years Foix worked trying to block the river at the point where it had changed from its original course, but every move met with failure. Vast amounts of money were invested until the 28th of October, 1578, when one last effort coincided with a storm. The dam held and the waters of the Adour rushed back into the old channel. The other course became silted up, and now only the lake at Hossegor remains. Bayonne was saved as a port, but even today continuous dredging is the price that has to be paid.

The English had been finally driven from Bayonne in 1451 when the French under their General Dunois attacked the town. The inhabitants resisted fiercely and successfully, but on August 21st a great white cloud surmounted by a crown which turned into a cross appeared over the port. The defenders amazed by the apparition thought that it was a sign from God, that they should wear the white cross of France and not the red cross of St George of England. Being of a realistic turn of mind they therefore surrendered. Superstition has always been a powerful weapon of war, but it has not often been so dramatically demonstrated as the so-called 'Miracle of Bayonne'. The inhabitants soon became disenchanted with French rule which turned out to be somewhat more fiscally strict than the English, and in later years they attempted several times to expel the French and return to English rule. These times, however, the elements did not intervene, and the French remained.

Bayonne has yet another side, for it is, and was, a city of chocolate. It was here that the Spanish and Portuguese Jews expelled from their homes in the sixteenth and seventeenth centuries came and settled. They brought with them the secrets of chocolate making which was up until that time an extremely bitter and seemingly unpleasant drink. The new blends and mixtures helped to make chocolate accepted and added to the prosperity of the town. Even today the excellent chocolate of Bayonne can be enjoyed here, eaten or drunk, as the fancy takes you.

After years of prosperity the Revolution brought hard times. The old rights of the free port were abolished and with the long wars against the English, trade declined. Bayonne did have one more brief period of military glory in 1814 when the victorious armies of Wellington marched out from the Pyrenees into France. Bayonne was once again besieged and once again resisted vigorously. The commander of the British besiegers the brilliant General Hope was even taken prisoner during a foray from the town. But all was in vain for Napoleon fell and Paris capitulated leaving Bayonne to try to fight a useless battle. Today the graves of some of the British troops that fell here can be seen in the cemetery of the Coldstream Guards just off the main road to Bordeaux.

As we have seen, Bayonne is of the Basque country but not really in it, but here is the richest of the Basque museums. A visit can give more of the feeling of the life of the Basques than months of travelling and visiting their land. There is a complete record of Basque history, how they lived and worked. There are complete reconstructions of their homes, their industries, their folklore.

One of the outstanding buildings of the town is the Cathedral of Ste Marie built in the thirteenth and fourteenth centuries in the Gothic style, more common in the north of France. At first it had only one tower, a second was added together with two steeples in about 1875. These, although charming from a distance, fail to balance with the older part of the building on closer inspection. The arms of England are engraved on the keystones of one of the vaults of the nave but no one seems to be able to explain their origins. The adjoining cloister is delightful, although much restored. The great west door suffered badly during the revolution, mostly it is claimed from the chocolate-brewing Jews who lived in the nearby St Esprit quarter of the town.

Not far from the cathedral is the Château Vieux, an old stronghold redesigned in the sixteenth century. Here the French knight Du Guesclin was imprisoned by the English whilst awaiting ransom. Each time he was captured he cost the French dear to regain their champion. Another ransom was paid here in 1530 by François I of France for the return of his two sons who had been held as security by Spain after the king himself had been captured at the battle of Pavia.

South away from Bayonne lies the heart of the Basque country while along the sea is the dramatic stretch of the Côte Basque.

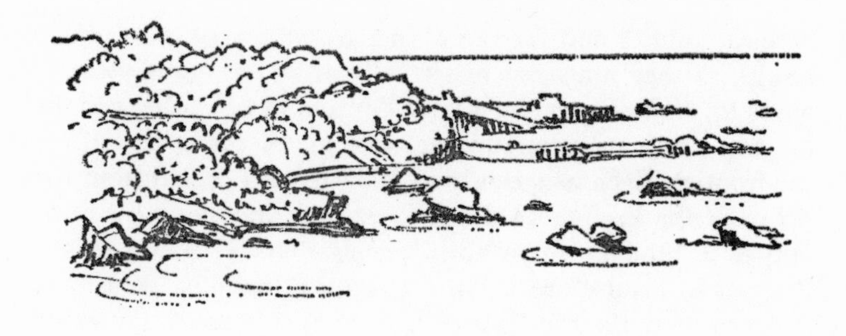

IV

THE COTE DES BASQUES

IF Bayonne is the gateway to the Basque country then Biarritz is its most treasured possession. It was the presence of an Imperial court that turned this modest fishing village into an international tourist resort which charmed kings and princes, attracted the rich, calmed the politicians and welcomed all. Here started that great flow of tourists that was to change the whole face of the coastal stretch of the land of the Basques. So much so that these independent people have become less known for themselves than for the delights of their vast sandy beaches and the thrills of the thundering Atlantic breakers being ridden by the daring surfers.

It has been thought that this influx of foreigners or Frenchmen from other regions would result in the breakdown of some of the Basque traditions and mysteries. But although along the coast itself some concessions may have been made to the needs of the tourist, one has only to look at the people as a whole to see that the national feeling of the Basques has never been so strongly marked. It has always been true to say that the Basques in France have had a deep feeling of involvement with their brothers over the frontier. The Spanish Basques seem to have had a much greater facility for involving themselves in

Spanish politics and for the most part with very unfortunate results, as they managed in virtually every case to ally themselves to the losing cause. Many Basques in Spain have made the trip north to escape to the welcome of the other side of the frontier. Even as recently as 1937 thousands fled from the defeat of the Basques in the civil war and the inevitable retribution it brought upon their people. Today, however, the Basques in France are making a stand in national politics. A stand to show their feelings of being a people apart, not easily to be assimilated into any facile centralised system.

Whether this movement is a purely local reaction or whether it is part of the world-wide movement of small proud peoples to mark their anxiety at the threat of being absorbed into ever larger units it is difficult to say. But it is true to say that as in Wales or Scotland or Brittany this effort is taking many forms. Usually this involves an obsession with the protection of the language, protection of old traditions and customs, a well-developed folklore and a development of native art and literature. All this has happened to the Basque under their green, red and white flag, which is itself but a recent innovation. It was in fact introduced in 1894 by Sabino de Arana Goiri the founder of the Basque Nationalist Party.

Ever since the earliest of recorded times the people that inhabited this coast have been fishermen living, fighting and dying on, for and by the sea that meant so much to them. Throughout the Middle Ages the whole of the Bay of Gascony was a favourite haunt of whales that came to sport themselves in its waters. The fishermen of Biarritz became the leading experts in the catching of the whale and from here came the most famous harpooners and whalers. Tall watch towers called *Atalyes* were erected along the coast, where men constantly looked out for the tell-tale spouts of the breathing whales. These *Atalyes* are still remembered in Biarritz by the Pointe d'Atalye, the headland near the fishing harbour. Once the look-outs saw whales, small rowing boats put out from all the nearby harbours carrying the eager harpooners towards the whales. Each harpoon was marked, so that when the animal was captured and beached it was divided according to the harpoons stuck into it. Whaling became such a profitable industry that the royal power soon realised that it could represent a good revenue, and promptly taxed all whales, that were caught. Other interests tried to extract a benefit from this trade particularly under the English rule. Even the chapter of Bayonne cathedral enjoyed a share. In 1498 when whales had already become scarce the church eventually gave up their twentieth share, but still claimed the tongue which was considered the greatest delicacy.

Finally the whales left the coast, decimated in numbers beyond sufferance. The last whale was caught at Biarritz in 1686, but already the whalers themselves, a determined adventurous race, had travelled far from the coasts of Gascony and hunted the whale off the coast of Scotland, Iceland and even north to Spitzbergen. Some crossed the seas to Newfoundland, which is perhaps the basis of the Basque claim to have discovered America before Columbus.

It was on these lengthy trips that they came into contact with other fishermen, Dutch, English, who soon realised the potential of the expert harpooners who sailed from the Basque coasts. These they invited to sail with them so that they could learn the mysteries of harpooning. However by the beginning of the seventeenth century these people had become rivals. The English and the Dutch closed their shores to the Basques, but the effect of this was mitigated by a certain Captain Sopite who discovered a system of melting the whale fat on board the ship. Three barrels of fat produced one barrel of oil, easier and lighter to transport. One boat could now carry the produce of seven whales from far-distant fishing grounds.

By now, too, another fish was attracting the Basque fishermen by its rich catches off the coasts, they had previously explored for whales, this was cod. The banks off Newfoundland were fished with great success and more and more Basque boats came to take part in this harvest of the sea. Once again the English were to menace the prosperity of the fishermen. At the end of the wars fought by Louis XIV the Treaty of Utrecht, in 1713, gave the fishing rights off Newfoundland to the English. Today only the small bleak islands of St Pierre and Miquelon remain of the great French enterprise in this part of the world. Here they still fish for cod, which is exported to France, but it is a declining industry and the boats find it difficult to find crews for their trips.

Little of this now remains, for Biarritz was to find its vocation in another way. As early as the beginning of the nineteenth century the people of Bayonne came to Biarritz riding on donkeys, sitting in special baskets one each side of the beast. Then in 1838 when the Spaniards were looking for a peaceful retreat from their own war-torn homeland the Countess of Montijo brought her daughter Eugènie for a short stay. They returned often, in later years and this exceptionally talented and attractive young Spanish girl was to have a dramatic effect on this small fishing village, and she herself was to have a dramatic and event-filled life.

Napoleon III, Emperor of France, creator of the Second Empire, of somewhat less-happy memory for the French than the First, was to be her husband. It is said that she missed her native Spain so much that she persuaded Napoleon to accompany her as close as possible to her homeland. Her memories of earlier stays made her choose Biarritz for these holidays. Napoleon, always ready to be charmed and led by his determined wife, became charmed by the Basque Coast and the couple returned many times. In 1855 Napoleon built his holiday home here the Villa Eugènie. It became a place to relax far from the troubles and affairs of state that weighed so heavily upon him. Here he enjoyed the privacy of family life and it is claimed, that when Bismarck came to stay here, he took away an impression that he had little to fear from the

French Emperor in his warlike ambitions which were to come to fruit in the year 1870. By now Biarritz had become fashionable and it attracted princes, their friends, the rich and the nearly rich from all over the world. Even the disappearance of the Emperor across the sea to England with his Empress, to whom Biarritz owed so much, was not to affect its new-found popularity. The new home that Napoleon found was to be by a strange fate in England, the country that had done so much to bring down his forbears. Later his son, the Prince Imperial was to die, as a British soldier fighting against the Zulus in Africa, a tragic and useless death. The palace they used at Chislehurst in Kent for many years still stands, but today it is the clubhouse for the local golf club.

Queen Victoria came to Biarritz in 1889 perhaps at the suggestion of the Empress to whom she had given shelter. Later her son Edward VII was to follow her example, staying at the Hotel du Palais which had grown from the original Villa Eugènie. One of its claims to fame is that it was here that the first British Prime Minister to be appointed on foreign soil to office when Asquith came to kiss the hand of Edward VII in 1908.

Biarritz has never really recovered the glories of those days. Rather like Britain, she has lost an Empire and has not yet found a new role. Biarritz today still has the feeling of the grandeur of its former existence, the imposing buildings, the wide streets, the dignified hotels all remain. Yet now the streets are full of darting motor cars and modern bright stylish shops, the beaches are strewn with families on holiday, while gay young people dare the waves in the balancing act of surf riding.

South of Biarritz the coast becomes rocky and steep cliffs overlook the sandy beaches. Here are small fishing villages now turned into holiday resorts, Bidart and Guethary are two of the best known. A little further south again is perhaps the most typical of the coastal towns of the Basques, St Jean-de-Luz.

The river Nivelle runs out, at last, into the sea past a huge sandy bay, which gives the impression of being virtually land locked. This is the safe quiet anchorage of St Jean-de-Luz, home of some of the greatest sailors of France. St Jean actually stands between the right bank of the river and the shore itself.

A town of great charm, full of narrow streets, tall elegant Basque houses and an indefinable air of adventure awaiting around the next corner, St Jean is still one of the leading fishing ports of France. As at Biarritz the fishermen suffered badly after the Treaty of Utrecht but they soon turned their activities to piracy and the corsairs of the coast swept the seas in their fast well-armoured privateers seeking for the slow heavily-laden merchant men. These more often than not were English which seems hard, for it was under the English rule that St Jean first began to prosper and its trade was protected by the English kings.

The corsairs or pirates were for many long years to trouble the English, and it is interesting to compare the tonnages of ships captured by the French with tonnages captured by the English during the Revolutionary and Napoleonic wars. The French proportion was the better by some twenty to one, but this was not due to the efficiency of the French navy at that time, but rather to the fact that the English enjoyed almost complete mastery of the seas, and her merchant ships sailed at will to trade all over the world, whilst French merchant ships had been swept from the seas completely at an early stage of the conflict. Some corsair captains were able therefore to claim large numbers of ships and some became famous, or notorious, according to taste. One of the best known was Etienne Pellot Montvieux who lived to the ripe old age of ninety years. Taken prisoner by the English several times, he claimed to have escaped on each occasion by his skill and courage. He later had a painting made of one of his exploits of boarding a powerful English ship from his privateer the General Augereau. The corsairs were under the general direction of Jean Dalbarde who also led a number of successful cruises and avoided the heavily armed battle ships of the English fleet.

Perhaps the most important event in the whole history of St Jean was the marriage there of Louis XIV and the daughter of the King of Spain. This union had been the subject of detailed negotiations by the French Minister Mazarin as part of the Treaty of the Pyrenees, 1659. The marriage took place on the 9th June 1660 and the houses where the King and his future wife stayed before their marriage are still standing, overlooking the port. In the church of St John the Baptist the magnificent ceremony directed by the Bishop of Bayonne lasted through the morning until three in the afternoon. The couple then returned to the House of the Infanta, whence they threw specially struck coins to the crowd below. After they had left the church, the door, that they had used, was bricked up so that no one else should have the opportunity of stepping through the same portal.

St Jean-de-Luz was now at the height of its prosperity but soon afterwards the decline of the fisheries began, then in 1749 the port was practically destroyed by a great storm, many houses were completely levelled and half the population fled. But there was soon to be some compensation for vast swarms of sardines appeared in the bay and the fishery industry was saved. Later the even more profitable tunny fishing was exploited and today St Jean is the main port of France for tunny fishing.

The old town is full of interesting houses. Apart from the Rue Gambetta or Grande Rue, as it is known, the Rue Mazarin has some fine Basque style buildings. Mazarin stayed here himself during the preparation for the royal marriage, and number two provided accommodation for the Emperor Napoleon I when he visited St Jean on his way to Spain. A short five years later Wellington was to use the same house when his army wintered in the Basque country in 1813–14. The port is always a place of attraction, often full of fishing boats and colourful sailors. Overlooking the harbour in the Place des Corsaires is the seamen's hostel, on its walls are carved the names of the local corsairs who once caused so much trouble to the Royal Navy. Across the harbour, on the far bank of the Nivelle, is the port of Ciboure, or Zubibura, the Basque name meaning the far side of the bridge. But now Ciboure is part of St Jean for the fishermen mostly make their homes across the river. Here there is a tradition of yet another strange race, who lived in Ciboure, the Cascarots; believed to be the result of mixed marriages between a tribe of wandering gypsies that made their way into the Basque country from Spain and either the ordinary local population which was already made up of many differing peoples or the strange Cagots, the untouchables of the Basques. These Cascarots have now, for all intents and purposes, disappeared, although some people claim that you may still stumble across a tall dark lithe man in the narrow streets of Ciboure, who is either a direct descendant or throw-back to those strange people. They had a tradition of outstanding physical activity, thinking nothing of running all the way to Bayonne loaded, with a heavy basket of fish on their heads and then running back with the empty basket the same day. Perhaps the truth of their origin will never fully be known for even in Basque their name *'kachkarot''* also applies to the bands of wandering dancers who once performed at every village carnival.

South again from St Jean-de-Luz and Ciboure is the last part of the French Basque coast, for Spain lies the other side of the estuary of the Bidassoa. Standing on its banks is the town of Hendaye, while a short distance away on the coast is Hendaye Plage, a recent development with what must be one of the finest beaches in Europe, a long stretch of soft golden sand. Set in the river is the Isle des Faisans which has played such an important role in French history. Today it no longer looks more than a flat mud bank in the river but once Kings and leaders met here. François I, captured at the battle of

Pavia, was exchanged here for his two sons, who went to be hostages for his ransom. The long and difficult negotiations for the Treaty of the Pyrenees were carried out here by Mazarin and, eventually, the treaty was signed in a beautifully decorated pavilion at the same time as the marriage contract between Louis XIV and the Infanta. The famous artist Velasquez was responsible for the decoration of the pavilion but he was to die soon afterwards, apparently from a chill caught whilst trying to complete the work.

Hendaye was originally a small town on the route to Santiago, the pilgrims' way; and there are still a number of old houses nearby the sixteenth century church of St Vincent whose tower once formed a look-out point for the whalers. In the Rue des Pecheurs is the house where the celebrated writer Pierre Loti lived and died in 1923.

Just a short distance upstream is the frontier village of Behobie and the pleasant typically Basque village of Biriatou, once a fortress of the Black Prince. The church is said to be the chapel of the Black Prince's castle and, in fact, it still has a Norman appearance.

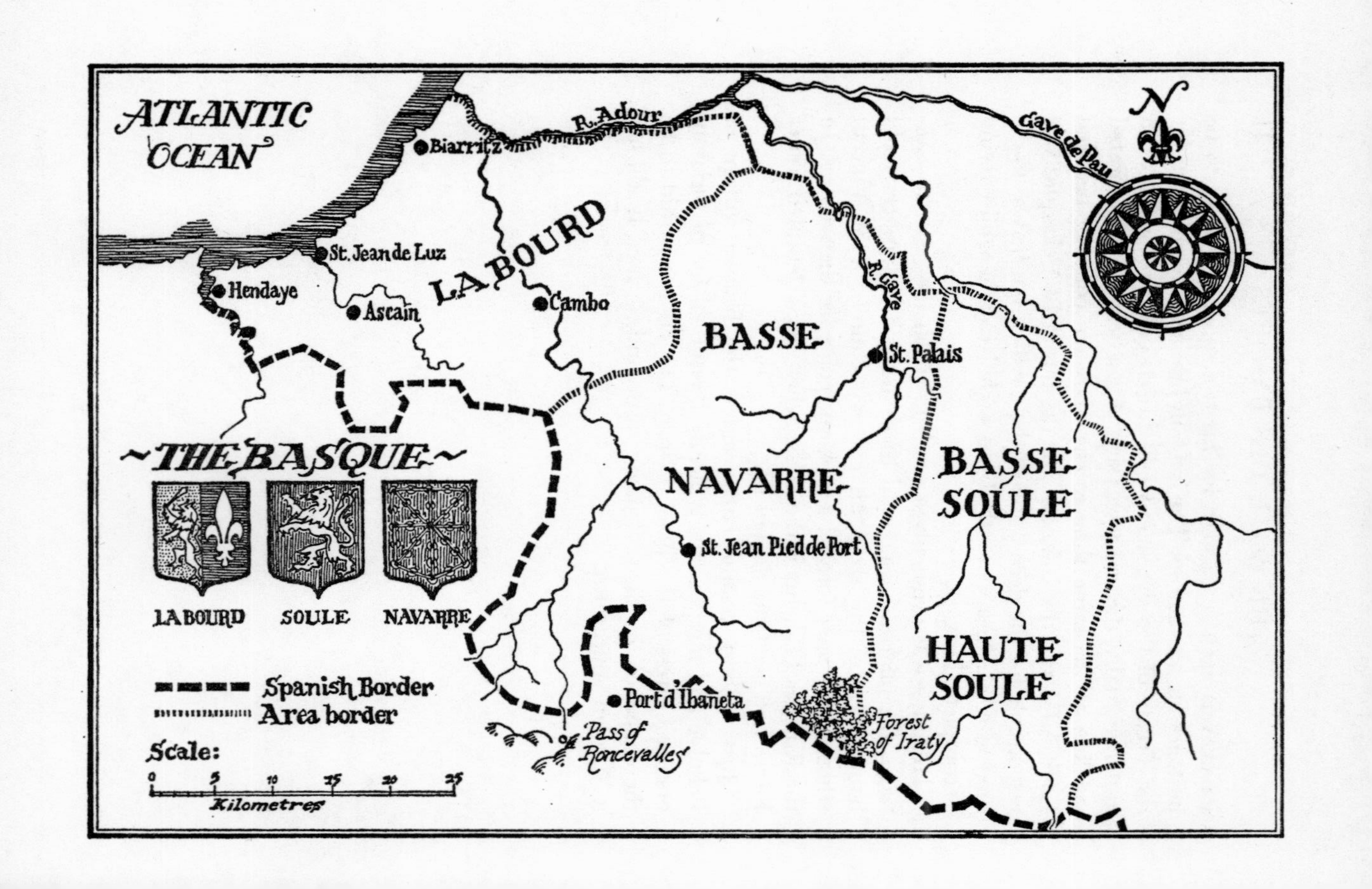

ATLANTIC OCEAN
N
Biarritz
R. Adour
Gave de Pau
St. Jean de Luz
Hendaye
Ascain
LABOURD
Cambo
BASSE
NAVARRE
R. Gave
St. Palais
BASSE SOULE
HAUTE SOULE
St. Jean Pied de Port
Port d'Ibañeta
Pass of Roncevalles
Forest of Iraty
~THE BASQUE~
LABOURD
SOULE
NAVARRE
Spanish Border
Area border
Scale:
0
5
10
15
20
25
Kilometres

V

THE BASQUE PYRENEES

THE whole of the coast south from St Jean-de-Luz sits under the almost menacing mountain of the Rhune climbing steeply from the coast, its angular shape makes it appear to lean over the surrounding countryside. The Rhune is the beginning of the Pyrenees proper stretching away from the wide sweeping beaches of the Atlantic to the small coves and rocky promontories of the Mediterranean coast some 270 miles away. If life along the coastal villages has always been under the influence of the sea, so inland the Basques have been people of the mountains, or have lived under their shadow.

Just inland from St Jean-de-Luz is a whole series of some of the most famous of Basque villages, set in rolling green countryside, where the Basques carry on their traditional agriculture and dairy farming. Here are the wide fields full of maize the sturdy light-brown cattle. Ascain is the first of these, and even today, it is full of old-style Basque houses all painted white. Here, too, stands the classic-style Basque church, for the Basques have a religious tradition, which remains firm. Village life is often centred around the church and the local priest has still the power and influence that he lost long ago elsewhere. The church is usually of a narrow straight nave surrounded by two or three tiers of galleries. For worship, only women are allowed into the nave together with children and the infirm, whilst the men remain in the galleries. The altar is always set up high and richly decorated. Often there is a small separate door for the use of the Cagots or untouchables. The cemetery surrounds the church, where the old round tombstones are often decorated with the Basque cross which resembles the inverted swastika. The origins of their emblem, like so much to do with these people, is completely unknown.

The houses are usually well built and face east so that they are protected as far as possible from the westerly gales and rains. The owner's name and the date of construction is carved over the door completely identifying the family with the house. The head of the household, the Etcheko Jaun, directs all facets of family life and his word is law. He even selects his heir, who is not necessarily the eldest son. The remaining children often leave home to work in other countries; many of the shepherds of South America are of Basque origin. Like most strongly national people they usually return home for long visits or for their old age.

Ascain has yet one other attraction, that of its pelota court or *fronton,* possibly the finest in the Basque country and visited by Queen Victoria and Edward VII during their visits to the coast.

Once again the origins of the game are difficult to trace, there seems to be no mention of it in any document before 1528, but Henry VII of England was reputed to have presented one hundred guineas to a famous player who performed before him. The game itself is basically simple, involving striking a ball against a wall with the hand. Similar games exist elsewhere. Originally the game was played with the bare hand and a ball made of wool bound with cotton. Later a smaller harder ball was used which needed a gloved hand.

The use of the *chistera* or basket to lengthen the hand and reinforce the strength of the throw did not become common until the second half of the nineteenth century. Nowadays, games take place using gloves, bare hands and the *chistera,* but this can vary from village to village. The use of a wooden bat to replace the hand is now rare. The players all dressed in white often look as if they are about to start an English village cricket match.

From Ascain the Col de St Ignace mounts rapidly, up towards the Rhune mountain. The col was named after St Ignace the founder of the Society of Jesus, the most dynamic of the catholic movements. From here, the Rhune mountain dominates and from its summit spectacular views reach far into the high Pyrenees. Now a peaceful mountain, with a mountain railway carrying thousands of visitors to its summit, it has a history as wild and bloody that surpasses the imagination. Many are the battles that have taken place here for the control its height gave. In the seventeenth century the men from the Bayonne regiment were fighting against the Spaniards when their ammunition ran out; showing great resource they tied their long knives on to the barrels of their muskets and charged down the slope sweeping away the enemy. Thus was born the bayonet which was to become such an important weapon in later years. The rocky outcrop that gave rise to this story is still known as La Bayonette.

But the Rhune has history of a darker kind for it was here that the witches, that play such a large part in Basque traditions were said to have met.

Although as we have seen the Basques were and are an extremely religious people, witchcraft seems to have played an important part in their lives for centuries. The first reports of witchcraft date back to 1450 when a convicted witch was executed for her crimes. But it was about one hundred years later that the Basques really became almost hysterically involved in witchcraft and black magic. Many factors may have been responsible for this; the new development of science, the religious controversies, political instability and not least the extreme poverty following the wars of religion. Thousands of witches, sorcerers and others now practised, or pretended to practise, their powers, mystery and magic were every day affairs; sickness of people or of cattle, successes or failure of crops, weather, fortune, happiness all was laid before the witches.

But there was a strong reaction from the central power, in 1576 the Lieutenant of the Bailly of Labourd summarily executed Marie de Chorropique, daughter of the house of Janetabaita and forty other witches. Thirty years later the situation had got so bad that King Henry IV sent a certain Concellor Lancre, of the Parliament at Bordeaux, to stamp out the practice of witchcraft. Although of Basque origin himself he set out on his task, which took from 2nd July to the 1st November 1609. During this period he questioned between sixty and eighty witches and some five hundred witnesses marked with the sign of the devil. They learned that some two thousand witches were involved in the various ceremonies, and to make an end of these, some six hundred people were said to have been executed. The curé of Ascain as well as the curé of Ciboure were unfrocked and burnt and five other priests were only saved after the intervention of the Bishop of Bayonne.

The early return of some five or six thousand sailors from Newfoundland and their anger at discovering the severe repression managed to stay some of the zeal of the inquiries, and eventually the threat of a Basque revolution caused the witch hunt to be abandoned. According to the report prepared by Lancre, whole villages took part in the rites usually in some inaccessible place like the top of the Rhune or the caves of Zugarramurdi, while four times a year there were even larger assemblies of up to twelve thousand people. These meetings were held on the coast, where Hendaye Plage now stands. Distance was no problem for the witches who only had to say the magic words Emen Hetan to travel rapidly out of the house by way of the chimney. The actual ceremonies corresponded to normal black magic procedure and no special Basque influence was noticeable, except for the names of the witches; Marie Dindarte of Sare, Saubadine de Subiette and Petri Daguerre of Ustaritz, Ansuperomin of St Jean-de-Luz and Ansugarto of Hendaye. These activities may have been exaggerated by the report, for Lancre did not hesitate to use torture and a simple denunciation by a child was thought sufficient proof. The traces of these activities remain in Basque folklore and tradition and even today they are considered to be a superstitious people.

Tucked in beneath the Rhune mountain is the village of Sare, one of the gems of the Basque country, full of old Basque houses and a charming rural atmosphere. Here, too, there is a fine *fronton* or pelota court, a typical Basque church with three tiers of galleries and a very rich altar. There is a fine war memorial of a man throwing a grenade over a figure of a pelota player. The town hall is a beautifully arcaded building overlooking the village square. But Sare has at least two claims to fame, the first has something to do with its geographical situation, some few hundred yards from the Spanish frontier. For Sare is known as the capital of the smugglers.

In these mountain areas there is a long tradition of smuggling and of a battle of wits with the customs officers. Never looked upon as a crime it is regarded rather as an extension of the principle of free trade. A network of forest paths make it easy to leave or enter either France or Spain, often without knowing exactly where you are. Along the frontier are a number of shops and bars on the Spanish side and it is relatively easy to drive or walk to them and buy drinks or souvenirs, without ever seeing a customs officer or immigration official. However, large scale smuggling is frowned upon and everyone will reassure you that such a thing no longer exists, but that if it did, it would involve very little in the way of the traditional brandy and liqueurs, cattle or even sheep, but rather electronic equipment, transistor radios and small pieces of engineering and mechanical parts. Stories may still be told of how great flocks of sheep were once passed across the border by decoying the customs from one point to another whilst the sheep were concealed in a border farm elsewhere.

There has also been a big demand from Spain for French drinks, even though they produce a good deal of wine and liqueurs themselves. During times of wars in either France or Spain, weapons, men and materials have all been passed. One story goes that at the time of the Carlist Wars a Basque carter arrived at the entrance of the village of Sare with his ox cart heavily loaded and covered with a sheet. He had travelled from St Jean-de-Luz with his load. He made his way along in the gathering dusk, prodding his oxen from time to time to speed them along, when suddenly he was halted by the Customs officers. Stopping his cart he leant on his stick and looked at the Officers.

'Well where are you going at this time of night' they asked, 'and what have you got there?'

'A piano,' he replied.

'A piano,' replied the officer, 'and who is it for?'

'It is for a big party being given by M. Abadie, they are certainly going to have a good time at the party and I am sure this infernal machine will make plenty of noise.'

'Off you go then,' said the Customs Officer, 'and take the piano to the party.'

Off went the carter into the night. In fact he was carrying a cannon for the Carlist forces across the frontier, who doubtless made plenty of noise.

For Sare's second point of interest we must turn to the unique Basque sport of *la chasse à la palombe*. This is a fantastic ritual trapping of these ring doves, which migrate across South West France every autumn in their thousands. Many are shot in the usual fashion of the French chasseur, but higher up in the mountain passes where the birds crowd together to navigate their way through the narrow gaps, huge nets are spread. First the birds have to be driven in the right direction by the beaters who are often concealed in trees or on piles of stones. Their shouts and waves drive the birds towards the narrow part of the pass, where the nets are secured between two trees. As the birds approach skilled men throw flat pieces of wood painted white that look rather like table tennis bats over the top of the massed flights of birds. The doves' great enemy is the hawk and when they see one they immediately dive for the nearest cover or at any rate get as near to the ground as possible to prevent the hawk swooping underneath them. They mistake the wooden discs for the hawks and dive straight into the almost invisible nets spread out in their paths. Sare is the centre of this sport and every autumn three or four hundred dozen are taken in this way. The totals are always counted in dozens for some unknown reason. Everyone in the village is an expert at some part of this sport, even the priests hurl the wooden discs with great skill over the flocks of birds. The trapping seems cruel but the birds can cause considerable damage to crops and their numbers have to be kept down by all possible means for they breed with great rapidity.

Across the river Nivelle is the next village, Ainhoa, which is quite outstandingly beautiful. A vast wide street with white painted old houses standing on each side showing off their painted shutters and flowered balconies. Here, again, are many examples of the houses bearing the name of the family and the date of construction carved into the stonework. The Maison Gorrita built in 1662 is marked as being erected by money sent home by a son of the house from the Indies so that it should not be sold to anyone else.

The next valley that leads into the Pyrenees is the Vallée des Aldudes through which the Nive des Aldudes, a fast-flowing stream, makes its rocky way. The word Aldudes means the high places and this valley was once the scene of a long drawn out struggle between the local inhabitants and the Spaniards living on the other side of the mountain pass. It was not finally settled until 1856 when a treaty settling the dispute over grazing rights was signed at Bayonne. Les Aldudes itself is a small place set in an open part of the valley. Here remains an interesting relic of the ill-fated Emperor Maximillian of Mexico, whom Napoleon III tried to set up as the ruler of that country. In fact he never really had any hope of achieving success and he was shot by the Mexicans at Queretaro in 1867. His personal possessions were auctioned. An expatriate Basque bid for his golden chaplet which he later presented to his home parish. It can still be seen on application at appropriate times.

St Etienne-de-Baigorry commonly known just as Baigorry has an old humped-backed bridge built back in 1661, which spans the Nive leading to the Château of Echau, home of one of the few noblemen who lived in the Basque country, the Viscount of Echau. At various times the Viscounts attempted to expand their local privileges but almost always without success, for the Basques as always vigorously defended their independence. The old forge was one of the bones of contention but it was finally shared half by the local people and half by the Viscount.

Just by the castle is the small collection of houses once the home of the Cagots or Basque untouchables. The Cagots raise yet another inexplicable problem. If we cannot trace the origins of the Basques themselves it seems almost an impossible task to explain their own mystery people.

The oldest Basque records refer to the Agotak or untouchables who were found all over South West France from earliest times. They certainly lived in Navarre in the early sixteenth century, for in 1514 the Cagots of Navarre applied to Pope Leon X to be relieved from the restrictions that were then imposed on them.

They received a reply which agreed to their pleas, but in

fact nothing happened in practical terms, until the nineteenth century. The Cagots, however, were not serfs as they had complete liberty under the jurisdiction of the church, which laid down that they should be excluded completely from normal community life. They were exempted from all taxes or dues, but were excluded from taking part in local life; they could not appear in public places, carry arms, sit with the faithful in church, kiss the cross, and finally on pain of death not to marry outside of their caste or even have what one Basque history book quaintly calls intimate relations. They were forced to wear a distinguishing mark, a badge in the form of a goose foot on their clothes.

Ownership of land was one of their privileges but if they produced crops or raised cattle they had to use them themselves, as they were not allowed to sell them. They were forced therefore into tasks as craftsmen, carpenters, masons and weavers. Eventually these occupations became theirs as almost of right.

Although there was some debate about their exact origin it seems likely that they were originally lepers, who had been kept away from the rest of the community so that their affliction should not spread. Over a period of hundreds of years this system proved effective. The most seriously sick were kept in special hospitals such as those provided by the Hospitaliers of St Lazarus, whilst those who showed the known signs of the disease, even hereditary ones, were forced to live in small hamlets away from the normal life of the community. Up until the end of the sixteenth century the Cagots were closely identified with this leprosy policy but slowly the marks passed from generation to generation disappeared. In time too their separation from the rest of the community was broken down, although in many parts this process was slow and there were many clashes between Cagots and the local people. Nowadays there is no trace of these people, although much of their past history remains. As we have seen, a low side door was provided for them in many Basque churches; their villages and hamlets still stand in some places. A strange fact is that often these areas once inhabited by the Cagots are now lived in by gypsies. Although no known link exists between the two peoples.

But the heart of the Basque country, the town of St Jean Pied-de-Port lies but a short distance to the east.

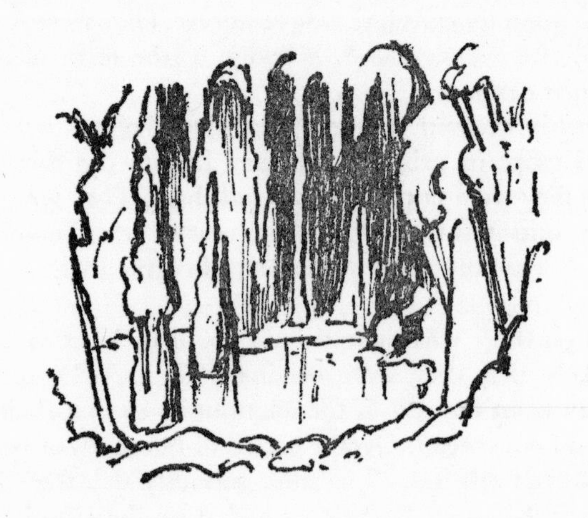

VI

IBANETA—THE WAY TO SPAIN

St Jean Pied-de-Port is now a quiet market town, except on market days when the streets are full of visitors, peasants, farmers and travelling salesmen. Here you can buy the traditional Basque cloth, coarsely woven in bright colours, local cheeses or, incongruously, mass-produced plastic toys. 'St John at the Foot of the Pass'—the most famous of all the passes into Spain, has come but slowly into the twentieth century, possibly because it still appears to feel the great weight of a long and turbulent history pressing upon it. Although a small settlement was established here in Roman times, the foundation of the town is attributed to King Garcia of Navarre in the eleventh century. It remained Spanish until the signing of the Treaty of the Pyrenees between France and Spain in 1659, when it was transferred to France and became the capital of French Navarre. Apart from a brief period at the time of the Revolution when, for secular reasons, its name was changed to Nive Franche, it has maintained its traditional role. The fortifications of the old or upper town date from the fifteenth century whilst most of the buildings in its steeply sloping streets are even more modern, dating from the sixteenth and seventeenth centuries.

The houses are built of red sandstone and, standing close together, they shelter the long climb to the centre-piece of the old town—the citadel. Nowadays, despite the refinements of the military architecture on display, the martial atmosphere has gone—it is hard to imagine the hurried ringing of bells announcing the coming of yet another band of pilgrims, on their way to the greatest shrine of the Middle Ages, St James of Compostella at Santiago.

St Jean Pied-de-Port was the last stage of the pilgrimage before the crossing of the Pyrenees into Spain, and here the pilgrims assembled in great groups, before climbing the pass to Roncevalles. This pilgrimage was one of the outstanding religious phenomena of this period, when religion was still the great driving force in men's lives. It is not clear why this particular journey should have been considered so worthwhile, for many thousands of people to leave their homes and relative security of their villages or towns and set forth across Europe to the small town of Santiago in Northern Spain. The story goes however that St James, the missionary who brought Christendom to Spain, was martyred in the Holy Land, where his body was placed into a small boat, which was then set adrift. This boat then drifted across the Mediterranean, out into the Atlantic and found its way to the same spot where St James had landed when he came to preach to the Iberians years before. He was buried there, but all trace of his tomb was lost, until some priests decided to look for it once again, led on by a star that moved across the sky to guide them in their task, they rediscovered the burial place and called it logically enough, the Campus Stellae. Santiago became the place of pilgrimage, here a sanctuary was built and all the facilities needed by the huge numbers of people were created.

As the pilgrims approached children would run down out of

the town to meet the weary grey-cloaked figures, all of whom would be carrying the traditional pilgrim's staff. Food was offered by the inhabitants as they passed by along the streets, where some pilgrims sought lodgings for the night. Most, however, continued to the Hospice in the Rue de la Citadelle which was maintained by the monks of Roncevalles, especially for the pilgrims. This was just one of the great Hospices that stood on the pilgrim routes, to provide shelter on the way. The church provided for all wants, spiritual and temporal, of the pilgrim. A strange sight the sombre pilgrims must have made when they left the town, for each cut himself a cross made of green leaves or branches and carried it up the road to the pass where it was laid down to decorate the Col d'Ibaneta, normally a bleak and rocky place.

But often all was not religious fervour, for one of the curses of the Middle Ages, the professional beggar, could not miss the opportunity of exploiting the pious pilgrims and often angry scenes ensued, notably when the beggars of St Jean itself found the competition from their itinerant brethren becoming too keen. The worst offenders would be hustled off to the Prison des Evêques, which stands still with the marks of the chains etched on its walls.

The pilgrims were possibly the first people to have a special guide book written for their use. The Codex de Compostella dating back to about 1140 was originally prepared by the monks of the great abbey of Cluny but appears under the name, possibly false, of Aymeri Picaud. It contained a mass of information, all useful, some perhaps exaggerated, speaking of St Jean Pied-de-Port; it warns pilgrims against the lawlessness of the local population, who were liable to fall upon them with heavy sticks and demand payment to let them pass and, if refused, would strike the pilgrims to the ground and make off with the money just the same. He went on to describe the inhabitants as swarthy, ugly, wicked, debauched, perverse, corrupt, drunken, violent, savage, cruel, empty of all good will and full of vice and iniquity. Quite a formidable list, but apparently it did not deter the pilgrims.

Through all these years pilgrims were the basis of the prosperity of the town and during the short summer months a continual stream would be coming or going on this compelling religious gesture.

After the sixteenth century, however, the pilgrims became few—to go to Santiago needed the authorisation of the King and the permission from a local priest. By this time too, men's thoughts were turning to other things more temporal and less spiritual.

The pilgrims were not the only travellers to pass this way, for many made a much sterner journey and many armies passed this gateway into Spain. Yet the pilgrims themselves might well have been responsible for one such military story, perhaps the best known of all, that of Roland, who fought and died in the Song of Roland, a *geste* or romantic tale of the Middle Ages peddled by the itinerant musicians or storytellers far and wide in those credulous times. Often these *gestes* were based on events or places of interest on the great pilgrimage routes and were used directly to incite more people to undertake the journeys and see the actual towns and places that had been mentioned.

Thus, then, was the Song of Roland conceived. Like most *gestes* little is known of its authorship or origins, but it is at least based on some fact, so that when the Norman soldiers began to chant the *geste* at the Battle of Hastings to rally their failing strength it was in the proper historical tradition.

In 778 Charlemagne led his armies on a great expedition into Spain, first he attacked Pamplona and then Saragossa, the first successfully, but at the latter, in a long struggle with the Moors he failed to gain the advantage and eventually was forced to withdraw. Taking his army back through the Pass at Roncevalles on the 15th August, 778, a date well established by historical evidence, the rearguard was attacked by the local people, the Basques of the area. Huge boulders and dead trees were hurled down upon the soldiers pinned in the narrow valley. The exact site, still remains unknown, although it is unlikely to be along the present road, which follows a different route from the old foot and mule tracks.

Charlemagne's rearguard, trapped as they were and encumbered with a large baggage train, were slaughtered by the attacking Basques; among those to die was Roland, Warden of the Brittany Marches.

The Song of Roland has taken these few facts and about them woven one of the most exciting and memorable of all epics. The attacking Basques have been turned into not less than three hundred thousand Moors, while the retreat itself followed a campaign of intrigue and excitement. Trapped by the Moors, the rearguard fights to the death and just when all is lost Roland attempts to shatter his famous sword, Durandel, upon a rock, but instead it splits the rock wide open. This rock can now be seen at Roncevalles or at Gavarnie some sixty miles away, according to personal choice. At last Roland is persuaded to sound his horn to recall Charlemagne to their aid, and he blows three great blasts, but the strain is so great that he bursts a vein in his neck and falls dead. Yet Charlemagne, over thirty miles away, hears the call and returns to avenge the heroes.

Today a car can make the journey over the pass from St Jean Pied-de-Port in minutes. The long climb up to the ridge which strained the last drop of religious fervour from the pilgrims is hardly noticed, just a little extra pressure on the accelerator pedal. At Arneguy the frontier is crossed and the first village of Spain, Valcarlos, lies tucked into the mountains overlooking the narrow Nive, that forms the actual boundary. The road crosses the Col d'Ibaneta, where a monument has been erected to commemorate the battle of 778, although this was unlikely to be the actual site either in fact or fiction. Roncevalles itself is a small collection of houses around the monastery, a long low building. Nearby stands the fine Gothic church with a squat tower, and its supposed relics of Roland and the Archbishop who fought with him. From Roncevalles the road falls away into Spain proper on the route to Pamplona.

In the footsteps of Roland through this pass have come many armies, mostly French, Spanish or Basque, yet it is perhaps once again with England that much of its later military glory lies.

VII

THE BLACK PRINCE

In February 1367 at the height of the Pyrenean winter the Black Prince led his so-often victorious Anglo-Gascon army over the Pass of Roncevalles on his way to Castile.

Ever since his great victory over the French at Poitiers the Black Prince had held court at Bordeaux where he ruled over his Duchy of Aquitaine. He was now thirty years old and years of hard campaigning, interspersed with the rich living, had left their mark on him. Also by now he was apparently as far from the throne as ever. His father Edward III ruled on in England still a powerful and dominating figure, who seemingly had banished his eldest son to the far off Duchy in France. But here the Prince was facing many problems, not least of these was the question of what to do about the so-called Free Companies. Aquitaine and the neighbouring French provinces suffered much since Poitiers from these bands of warriors. Great groups of soldiers, English, French and German harried the countryside for hundreds of miles around, threatening even the Pope in the temporarily holy city of Avignon. The war between France and England had now continued for so long that thousands knew no other calling but war, and during the periods of temporary peace or general military inactivity they were willing to turn their arms to any enterprise.

Charles V of France, who had succeeded the unhappy John, who spent so much of his reign a prisoner of the English, was shrewd and was obsessed with the idea of avoiding the fatal clash of pitched battle with the English, that had proved so disastrous to his forbears. He chose therefore to wear down the English power in France by other means. When Pedro, the so-called Cruel King of Castile, was arraigned before the Pope, Charles aided Henry of Transtamare, Pedro's bastard brother, to claim his throne. Betrand du Guesclin, Champion of France, hastily ransomed once again from the English, was appointed to rally his comrades in the Free-Companies and take them to Castile, whence Pedro, who now found himself without an army, was forced to flee. Charles knew that the Black Prince would not easily accept that the new King of Castile should be a friend of the French and consequently a menace to his southern border.

Pedro now made his way to the court of the Black Prince at Bordeaux, where in this age of chivalry he knew that his case would not go unheeded. The Black Prince heard his pleas with eager ears for at last he saw the opportunity for another of his glorious campaigns. Despite opposition from his advisers and the Parliament of Aquitaine the Prince obtained a reluctant permission from his father in England to take up Pedro's cause. His advisers argued that to launch his army over the Pyrenees into Castile was just what Charles of France wanted, so that he could attack and perhaps capture some of the border fortresses with relative impunity.

But the Prince was not to be swayed, and moving court south to Bayonne, he commenced preparations for the invasion. He assembled a large Anglo-Gascon army at Dax and prepared to cross the Pyrenees into Castile. Two problems faced him, one was the acute winter weather and the second was that the passes of the Pyrenees were under the control of another Charles, King of Navarre. The second of these had to be resolved immediately, and, at once, the Prince sent his brother Duke of Lancaster and his leading adviser, Sir John Chandos to St Jean Pied-de-Port to negotiate the passage of his army. It was agreed that Charles would allow the passage of the English in return for a substantial cash payment. But Charles, not being sure of the final outcome, took the precaution of negotiating also with Henry of Transtamare to keep open all his options. He was, however, compromised when a largely English force of Free-Companies under Sir Hugh Calverly appeared on the southern side of the pass, seized and burnt two Navarese towns of Miranda del Arge and Puenta la Reine. Charles of Navarre suitably intimidated, opened the passes and swore to aid the Prince in his mission to replace Pedro on the throne of Castile. Now at last the Prince could move, just two days after his wife, Princess Joan of Kent, had presented him with another son, later to be the ill-fated Richard II.

Bertrand du Guesclin was in turn taken by surprise, for he was still ensconced comfortably in Provence with the bulk of the Free-Companies, who had just returned with him from placing Henry on the throne of Castile. He had not anticipated that the Black Prince would attempt the crossing in winter or, above all, that Charles of Navarre would stand aside and grant free passage. Rallying his forces and calling in the Free-Companies once again he set out for Castile in great haste, to arrive before the formidable army of the Black Prince.

The English army was some twenty thousand strong, half men at arms and half archers, and included a formidable array of the great knights of those chivalrous times. Forcing their way up the pass from St Jean Pied-de-Port they struggled through heavy snow past Roncevalles, urging on their tired horses and pushing their carts and supply wagons. The cold was intense and some doubted if ever the army would win free of the stern mountains of the Pyrenees. Yet the planning and enthusiasm of the Prince and his chief counsellor, Sir John Chandos, overcame the natural difficulties and the army at last made its way down the rather more gently sloping road to Pamplona. It took three days for the army to make the passage, knights, men-at-arms, archers, Free-Companions, all cold, weary and discouraged, for there but a short way ahead at Burgos was a strong army under Henry Transtamare.

For three weeks the Black Prince hesitated whether to attack or to face an ignominious retreat. His army suffered even more depredations from the cold and disease. Don Tello, brother of King Henry, made a surprise night attack upon the English camp with a force of some six thousand cavalry. He managed to do some damage to the English and was only driven off after a sharp fight. As he withdrew at dawn, his troops met a foraging party of English returning to their camp. Although only about four hundred strong, half men-at-arms and half archers, they refused Don Tello's order to surrender and fell back upon a small hill, the hill of Arniz. All day they held the hill against the six thousand Castilians and French, and, as many times before, the English archers caused great slaughter amongst the attacking knights, shooting their war horses from under them. The Castilians would not accept the advice of the French to fight on foot, which they felt to be below their station in the ranks of chivalry. It was not until the Marshal of France d'Audenham, who had fought at Poitiers, formed up a thousand of the remaining knights on foot to charge the remnants on the hill that at last the crest was carried. It is said to this day the hill is known as the hill of the English.

It was, in fact, just one more piece of evidence of the outstanding power of the English army in the pitched battle—the power based on the long bow.

The Prince now decided to turn the flank of the strong Castilian position and by a long dangerous and militarily risky march, lead his army in a straggling column across the hills of

Cantabria to Logrono on the river Ebro. He then crossed the river and marched on to the town of Navaretta.

Henry was forced out of a strong defensive position to move his army to follow the English to the nearby village of Najera. Du Guesclin advised the King to retreat to a better position, so as to force the English in turn to attack under unfavourable conditions, but the pride of Castilians prevented any such manœuvre.

On April 3rd, the Black Prince rode out with his army to what was to be his third great victory—but also his last. Once again the English archers shot their way to victory, the horses of the Castilian knights, the genetours or light cavalry, the slingers, the Genoese crossbowmen, the French knights on foot, all went down before them. The two wings of the Castilian army gave way and soon the main body was surrounded and crushed. Henry himself broke free, but most of the rest of his own and the French knights, who had come to join him died, or were captured where they stood. Here the unfortunate Du Guesclin was again seized by the English having been but lately ransomed, after being made a prisoner at the battle of Auray.

The French having been left on the field suffered badly and afterwards it was claimed that the problem of the Free-Companions that had troubled France and Aquitaine for so long was solved at Najera—they all lay dead on the battlefield.

After the success of the battle, troubles fell fast upon the Black Prince. Pedro failed to provide the money and supplies he had promised, men fell to disease in their hundreds and the Prince himself contracted the dysentery that was, in time, to kill him. Eventually sick in body and spirit the army painfully retraced its steps to the Pyrenees and Roncevalles. The Black Prince could no longer stay in Spain for his own Duchy was being threatened by the French, taking the opportunity offered by his long absence. However, it was hardly a conquering army that made its way down to St Jean Pied-de-Port eight short months after leaving so hopefully in the opposite direction.

From this point in time English power in Aquitaine and eventually in all France, was to decline. The Spanish adventure was, in many ways, the beginning of the end of the Hundred Years War, due to drag wearily on for many years yet. But the English were to come again to Roncevalles and down the pass to St Jean Pied-de-Port, but this time a vastly different army in another age.

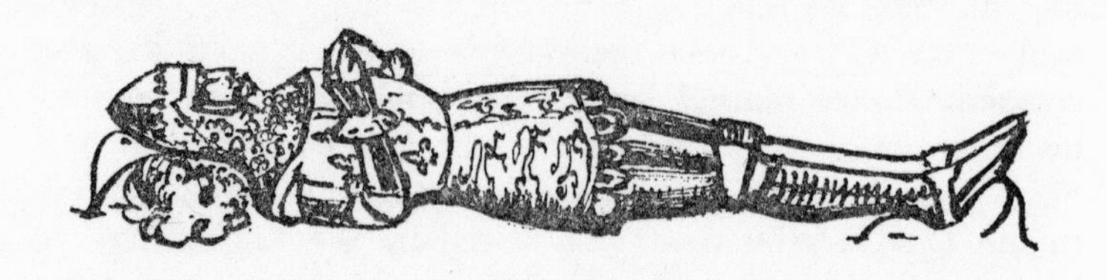

VIII

THE BASQUE INTERIOR

BEYOND St Jean Pied-de-Port is one of the wildest and least known parts of the whole of the Basque country. The road up to Mendive is open to all traffic, but from there it is preferable to use the jeep services up the rapidly climbing tracks past the Chapel of St Sauveur, a small place of pilgrimage in the mountains, and up to the Col Burdin Curutcheta. Here is the wild untouched forest of Iraty. Now a state forest full of giant beech trees, once used to make oars for galleys or charcoal for furnaces, they remain for the most part as they have for centuries past. The difficulties of access have held back the commercial exploitation of the timber, also the local rivers are not capable of providing enough water to float the giant trees down to the lower slopes.

Here animals of all kinds once roamed freely, wolves have now disappeared, but perhaps the largest of all the Pyrenean animals, the bear still hides away in the deepest darkest places of the woods. The bear comes out only rarely and always hides away from man. From time to time evidence appears of the continued existence of bears, not only here but further east in the High Pyrenees themselves.

The forest is still to a large extent managed by a syndicate of the communities of the surrounding areas, even though it does in fact stretch across the frontier into Spain.

Further east again is the still wild valley of the Saison. Here the Saison or Mauleon torrent pours down into the Gave d'Oloron. Above Licq the valley splits into two parts, the valleys of the Larrau and the Uhaitxa and this is perhaps the most dramatic part of this mountainous region—great sharp rocks and cracks run down the face of the mountains. Every year in August one of the most terrifying of all motor rallies takes place here. The Rallye des Cimes, when small jeep-style vehicles race over the mountain tracks and even what appear to be no tracks at all.

At the head of the valley of the Uhaitxa are the famous Gorges de Kakouetta. Access to the Gorges can be difficult if the water level is high, but it can usually be successfully completed in summer. The entrance is through the Grand Etroit, a narrow gap only some ten feet wide but over six hundred and fifty feet deep. The path involves wading through the water at several points and leads to a spectacular waterfall.

Higher up the valley is the shepherd's village of Ste Engrâce with its interesting church with a fine Romanesque style porch. Ste Engrâce was a Spanish saint martyred in Saragossa and is now remembered in this little church high up in the French Pyrenees; why this should be, no one quite seems to know.

Perhaps the most picturesque village of the valley is the rather larger community of Tardet Sorholus. A local market centre, it is full of charming houses, some with the typical arcades. Tardets is near to the Chapelle de la Madeleine, which is the destination of a local pilgrimage, it also enjoys fine views over the surrounding countryside.

Tardets' main interest is in that it is a centre for Basque traditions, particularly the well-known Basque dances and the so-called pastoral plays. The Basques have a great tradition of folklore and it is in many ways an overt expression of their strong group and racial feelings. The fact that they have been so well preserved is of itself significant. The dances are spectacular and performed in different villages whenever there is a festival of some kind or another. The music for the dances is provided by two weird instruments the *tchirulari,* a three-holed flute, and the *ttunttun,* a local form of the tambourine. The group is usually divided into two parts, the reds who are the leaders, and the blacks who, in fact, are just a parody of the expert dancers of the reds.

The reds travel along the roads on their way to the fête using the special step that has passed into classical ballet as the Pas de Basque. They are composed of Tcherrero, wearing a belt adorned with bells and carrying a stick like a horse's tail; the Gathuzain, the cat man, carrying what are known as witches scissors, he creeps and bounds along simulating the movements of a cat; the Kantiniersa, part man, part woman; the Enseinari carrying the ensign or flag. Then comes the hero of the occasion the Zamalzain who is both horse and rider; he prances along as if he were actually riding the wicker-framed horse, that is part of his costume. The troupe is completed by the Jauna eta Anderea, the lord and his lady; the Laboria eta Etcheko anderea, the ploughman and his wife, and some minor figures. The blacks, however, include the same characters, but a rather mixed collection of gypsies, tinkers and other itinerant salesmen dressed in sheets decorated in simple style.

On arrival at the village the dancers first have to force an entrance through a series of barricades, which fall quickly after a few dance steps have been performed. Then the group visit the most important citizens, where after performing, they are suitably refreshed and continue to the main square for the performance. The reds begin with a long series of traditional dances known as the *bralia* which concludes with the spectacular *godalet dantza,* the dance of the wine glass. In this dance a glass full of wine is placed on the ground while they cavort around and over it without actually spilling a

drop. This in turn is followed by a series of less-formal dances in which the blacks get an opportunity to show some humour, and the evening is completed by a general dance for everyone. Tardets is often the scene of friendly competition between the groups or *mascardes.*

The plays often take the form of pastorals or Tragedies and again it is the young men and the boys of the village who are the actors. The plays always follow roughly the same story and format, although they may be varied from time to time by local authors. It is always the good, who finally triumph, after much difficulty over the bad. Usually this means victory for the Christians over the Moors, the Christians wear blue and the Moors red. The play opens with a long sermon explaining the theme of the play, while a second sermon comes at the end as a sort of epilogue or even a vote of thanks. In between the action may last for hours, often all day, the actors make little pretence at acting but rather recite long speeches clarifying their role and deeds. Great emphasis is placed on the proper presentation of these speeches including perfect diction. The battles are mere gestures and if one of the leading actors is killed his comrades quickly place a sheet on the floor for him to fall into so that his elaborate costume is not soiled by touching the ground.

North from the valley of the Saison is the road back to Bayonne and the coast. St Palais is an important market centre, its charter to hold a market dating back to the fifteenth century. It was also a centre where numbers of itinerant gypsies came and settled after being expelled in the sixteenth century from Spain along with the Jews, who, we saw, settled in Bayonne. For many years they were oppressed by the Basques. They were suspected of being responsible for much of the smuggling that took place over the frontier and also of being involved in black magic which was to bring so much distress to the Basque people.

However, despite attempts to transport them to the colonies

and other dire threats they remained and wandered no more. They took up their trades of charcoal burners, tinkers, weavers, etc. Today they have lost their original tongue amongst the Basque and French now used, but physically they still remain of the original gypsy stock, for they have never intermarried with the local population outside of perhaps some of the cagots or untouchables.

Hasparren is a small industrial town set amongst pleasant rounded hills. It dates back to the times of the Romans but it carries a Basque name, which means in the heart of the oak, which sounds a very British connotation. Once the whole area was covered with great forests of oak, now all have gone, but the tanneries that depended on the products of the oak bark still remain. Hasparren is still a leather production centre and in particular it is noted for its fine shoe leather. Not far away are the remarkable caves of Isturits and Oxocelhaya, here there are prehistoric drawings of many animals but notably salmon and horses. Stalactites and stalagmites abound and form many strange and wondrous shapes.

Further on the road to Bayonne is the small town of Ustaritz, built largely in more recent times, it shows how town planning can preserve the old styles of building by insisting that new developments should be in the traditional fashion. Here is the Seminary of St François-de-Larressore founded in 1753, which is responsible for education of the Basques in their own language and traditions. It has played a remarkable part in preserving the old Basque language as a living entity. Once the town was the Parliament of Labourd and the mayors of all the towns in the province used to meet here at the Château de la Motte. This meeting known as the Bilcar was only for the ordinary people, all priests and nobility were excluded.

Before returning finally to Bayonne it is worth while stopping at the old feudal town of Espelette. Now a rather large somewhat scattered village on the Laxa, a tributary of the Nive, its main industry is farming, but once it was an important iron-ore mining and porcelain production centre. It was here too that in 1828 was the last recorded occurrence of the old Basque customs of the *charivari*, which is in truth, yet another manifestation of their strong desires to maintain the old system and not to accept change for its own sake. The *charivari* is used for any local scandal, such as the marriage of an older

man with a young wife or a man who was dominated by a shrewish wife. In Espelette it was recorded as the case of a Catholic girl who married a Protestant. The form of the *charivari* was that of a nocturnal serenade with apt words, according to the situation and music supplied by cow bells, cow horns and saucepans. This rather cruel custom no longer exists in its original form, but in some places a rather minor version is reputedly sometimes practised.

Only a few miles away is the village of St Pée-sur-Nivelle,

of little interest today, but it was here that Joseph Bonaparte fled in 1813 after he had been crushingly defeated by Wellington at the battle of Vittoria. Disgraced and disillusioned and virtually penniless, for he had lost all his baggage and only just escaped capture by the British. He waited to hear what fate his brother had in store for him. He soon found out, when Marshal Soult arrived with orders to replace him immediately as commander of the French Army in the Pyrenees.

Soult was a tough professional soldier and the French army was still relatively strong and the main passes of the Pyrenees were still in his hands, but could he hold them against the fast-moving Wellington?

IX

THE BATTLES OF THE PYRENEES

By July 1813 the Duke of Wellington had brought a British army across the whole of the Spanish Peninsula to the line of the Pyrenees and the very edge of France itself. Although this campaign had been going on for many years, it was only now after a series of remarkable victories that Wellington was in a position, where he was at last able to threaten the Empire of Napoleon directly.

After the defeat of his brother at Vittoria, Napoleon although menaced strongly on his eastern frontiers, had to take drastic steps to hold the line of the Pyrenees, to prevent an invasion from that direction. As we have seen he sent one of his marshals, Marshal Soult, as he himself was unable to leave his even more urgent problems. Soult took command as soon as he arrived, and with his usual drive commenced to prepare his badly shaken army for the tasks that lay ahead. He reorganised the remnants of the army from Spain, mobilised all local troops and brought in the garrison troops from all over South West France. Soon he had some one hundred thousand men under arms. Meanwhile another French army under Marshal Suchet was still in the eastern provinces of Spain, so that, in fact Wellington was very nearly outnumbered. In addition, Wellington's army was made up of men of three nationalities, British, Spanish and Portuguese. The British element being only some thirty seven thousand strong.

Within a short time Soult had changed his army back into an effective fighting force and was busily planning some offensive action to try to relieve the defenders of the two strongholds of Pamplona and San Sebastian, that were still holding out in Spain. The troops needed to carry out these siege operations made it impossible for Wellington to force through the mountain passes, and, in fact, he was very much on the defensive at this stage of the operation. The Pyrenees running roughly east west and the passes being cut off one from the other made intercommunication and rapid movement extremely difficult. This meant in turn that most troops had to be committed forward rather than in a rear position, which would have enabled them to move quickly to any part of the front which was being threatened.

Soult planned to attack the right-hand flank of the British position in strength, in the hope that he would force a passage, before superior numbers could be brought to bear against him. Also it meant that he would be able to relieve Pamplona, which he knew to be nearing the end of its resistance, whilst San Sebastian seemed to be in better condition. If he succeeded and broke through to Pamplona he would be in a position to roll up the British from the flank and rear, division by division.

The British right was in the pass of Roncevalles under General Byng, while a Portuguese division was based on Usepel in the Aldudes. They were supported by the Fourth British division under General Sir Lowry Cole and the famous Third British division under their determined commander General Sir Thomas Picton. Against them Soult moved two Corps, the First Corps under General Clausel and the Second Corps under General Reille, both were assembled around St Jean Pied-de-

Port. A Third Corps under General D'Urlon was held in reserve ready to exploit the breakthrough, and the Fourth Corps were engaged on keeping the centre and left of the British occupied.

Although heavy rain and floods delayed the French movement on the 24th July, sixteen thousand men under Clausel attacked one thousand six hundred under Byng in the Roncevalles pass. At the same time Reille attacked on his right and despite strong resistance by Campbell and the arrival of Cole's supporting division the British were forced back. But the French failed to follow up this success and harass the British before they could concentrate in sufficient numbers. For some five hours on July 26th Cole was exposed to the whole weight of Soult's army, but the attack never came, Reille and Clausel claimed that they were held up by fog and mist and lack of local guides. Cole took the opportunity to make good his retreat to join up with Picton.

When the news of the French attack came Wellington was far away to the West at San Sebastian. He made his way quickly towards Pamplona moving all available troops in the same direction. He soon had the Sixth, Seventh and the famous Light divisions all on the way towards the critical area. In the meanwhile General Picton formed a line on the heights of St Christobal in front of Pamplona. Soult realised that he must attack this position as soon as possible, for time was on the side of the British, however, he delayed whilst reconnaissance was made. Wellington now had arrived on the scene himself accompanied by only one staff officer Lord Fitzroy Somerset, later Lord Raglan, famous in the Crimean War.

On July 28th the French attacked having realised that strong British reinforcements would soon arrive. Clausel attempted to turn the flank of the ridge but the Sixth division arrived in time to trap him against the main body of the British army. The rest of the French under Reille attacked the steep heights from the front, an almost impossible task. Four times the French attempted to storm the ridge but each time were beaten back. In the last attack the troops were so tired that it is reported that the French officers were seen to pull their men up the hill by their belts. This ended the action and the French withdrew.

The next day Soult attempted to hold the British with a small force while he fell back behind the town of Sorauren so that he could make an orderly retirement upon the passes of the Pyrenees and his own reserves. Wellington, however, attacked Sorauren and two French divisions were caught on the move and virtually broken as fighting forces. Now followed a series of attempts to get between the French and their route back over the mountains, but at last, Soult won free and his badly decimated army straggled back to the frontier.

Now Soult had to rebuild his forces into an army once again, while he watched powerless as the British increased their pressure on San Sebastian. Having failed on the British right he now decided to use the same tactics, a rapid concentration of force against their left. Clausel and Reille once more moved to the attack but the British positions were strongly placed on the San Marcial heights. The main strong point was held by a Spanish division, which held on only with great difficulty. But Wellington had now started a movement to outflank the French by moving his strong right wing forward. The news of this movement together with confirmation that San Sebastian had fallen the same day decided Soult to withdraw once again. Nature now intervened, for a great storm swept over the battlefield and under its cover Reille's division was able to get back safely behind the Bidassoa. Clausel's division was less fortunate, for the river had risen rapidly to flood levels and many of his men failed to get across, at what had once been easy fords. The losses of this attack finally decided Soult that his offensive opportunities had now come to an end and that he must concentrate on defence of the frontier.

Wellington now had to face the problem of the attack. His troops had to be reorganised, prepared and trained for the operations to follow. Soult with his usual energy had organised two main strong points in his defence line, at Bayonne and St Jean Pied-de-Port and linking the two was a system of prepared defensive positions and entrenchments. These defences were particularly strong along the river Bidassoa and around the Rhune mountain and these two natural features menaced all forward movement. It was planned therefore to attack both at the same time in the early days of October.

The two Generals who seemed to bear the brunt of all these actions, Clausel and Reille, were again to be involved. Clausel had his men established in a series of redoubts to hold the Rhune while Reille's division covered the two ridges, that ran from the mountain to the sea along the north bank of the Bidassoa. The British army was still spread out between Roncevalles and the sea. A Spanish division with the Light Division was near to the Rhune while along the south bank of the Bidassoa were another Spanish Division, the First and Fifth divisions and two independent Brigades, one British under General Aylmer and one Portuguese under General Wilson. The Spaniards were to attack the Rhune while some twenty four thousand British troops were to attempt to storm across the Bidassoa, a most desperate plan, where there were no bridges and the few fords were covered by artillery fire. In addition the French were very strongly placed high up overlooking the river from the escarpment on the northern bank.

Wellington's plan was to attack on the 7th October at the very mouth of the river where at low tide a broad stretch of sand half a mile wide was exposed. Just before dawn there was a severe storm which helped to conceal the movement of the English troops, and the First and Fifth divisions crossed the sands without a shot being fired and assaulted the large French redoubt known as the Sans Culottes and Hendaye itself. Once established, a rocket fired from the steeple of the church at

Fuenterrabia signalled the British artillery to cover the advance of the remainder of the attacking force against another series of redoubts, the Louis XIV, the Café Republicain and the Croix des Bouquets. The first two of these were soon taken but the third held out strongly, but eventually it is reported that Colonel Cameron the commander of the Ninth Regiment led his men straight into the position with 'astonishing courage'. Meanwhile the Fifth Division pressing towards the Sans Culottes now menaced the whole of the French right flank. Reille who was in command decided on retreat, which was only saved from becoming a rout by the timely arrival of the reserve division under General Villate. The forcing of the river Bidassoa was one of Wellington's outstanding achievements, for with very few casualties, he forced the French out of a strong well-defended area. It was as the historian of the Peninsula War, Napier, said a 'truly stupendous operation'. For if the first assault had failed then the British would have been isolated on the wrong side of the river by the returning tide.

Meanwhile, a great struggle was taking place for the Rhune mountain. Under General Taupin the French held the hill with the high ground that ran down to the river. First a small hill, the Dos d'Ours was assaulted by the British while the Spaniards under General Girons fought their way up the main mountain. The French made good use of their height and progress was slow. However, the story goes that the *aide-de-camp* of General Alten, a young officer named Havelock who had come with a message for Girons, seeing that the Spaniards were held up dashed forward and led the tired troops up the steep slope forcing the French back to the very summit. Here they held out throughout the night.

The next morning the Sixth Division moved to outflank the mountain and Clausel pulled back his men behind the Nivelle. He left a brigade on the Lesser Rhune and a heavily defended position in the village of Sare. On the right of the French

Reille held another strong position in front of St Jean-de-Luz, in deep entrenchments between Ascain and the sea. These defences were so strong that they were compared to the lines of Torres Vedras, that Wellington himself had prepared around Lisbon nearly three years earlier. In addition a strong force was established on the left under d'Erlon to guard that flank. This part of the line was less well fortified and it was here that Wellington decided to attack, for if he could break through he would outflank the position that Reille held on the coast. Throughout the month of October the British made their pre-

parations and in the first week of November they were ready to attack. General Sir Rowland Hill moved against D'Erlon with the Second and Sixth Divisions, so as to force him back towards Ainhoa, while General Sir William Beresford with a very powerful force of British and Spaniards assaulted the strongpoint at Sare, in an attempt to split the forces of D'Erlon and Clausel. The Light Division were to attack Ascain and General Sir John Hope had the task of keeping Reille occupied so that they could not reinforce their left.

The first attack was against the Lesser Rhune, which was soon seized by the 43rd Regiment, who moved on against Ascain. The Fourth Division, under the direction of General

Cole, advanced against Sare and stormed it with great verve using ladders to scale the defences. General Hill also proceeded to drive the French out of Ainhoa and forced the gap between Clausel and D'Erlon, who was then attacked in great strength. He fell back towards St Pée to avoid being cut off from the main body of the French. The central positions under Clausel were now menaced and the Light Division broke through the French under General Taupin who were already weakened by the fearsome sounds of battle from their rear. Now the British were in a position to roll up the whole French army piecemeal division by division from Ascain to the sea. Soult, making a rapid appreciation, quickly pulled back Reille's troops from their now impossible situation and the great entrenchments which the French had spent so much time and effort to build were abandoned without a fight. The Battle of the Nivelle, as this action was to be called was a a sorry defeat for the French who lost some fifty guns and five thousand men in killed, wounded and prisoners.

The French were now established behind the river Nive, and by December, Wellington had decided to force a crossing of the river. He chose first to cross by the ford at Cambo and the bridge was still standing at Ustaritz. A complete Corps, under the command of General Hill, moved against these points supported by another corps under General Beresford. Meanwhile General Hope led his troops up as far as the outer defences of the city of Bayonne. He was the first to be attacked by the French who were able to concentrate their forces against him without difficulty. Hope however was able to maintain his position and Soult moved his counter attack to Hill's troops near Cambo and Ustaritz, where they had forced the crossings but as yet were not firmly established. Wellington moved quickly to support the exposed Hill, who came under increasingly powerful French counter attacks and on December 13th a sharp and bloody battle took place at St Pierre. The French attacked vigorously for they knew that if Hill was not pushed back across the river the whole flank of their position, that hinged on Bayonne, would be turned. Despite a long series of reverses the French had not lost their well-known verve in the attack and for some hours the result of the battle hung in the balance. It was only the speed with which the British could move up their powerful reserves that finally decided the outcome. According to Napier, Wellington said that he had never seen a field so thickly strewn with dead; nor could the determination of the combatants be well denied when five thousand men were killed and wounded in three hours upon the space of one mile.

The winter weather then prevented any further exploitations of this success until February 1814 and for the remainder of December and for the month of January both armies moved into winter quarters. But the great battles that ravaged the Basque country were not yet over. In February Wellington decided that the moment was ripe for a direct assault on Bayonne itself. Hope's Corps had the task of forcing the Adour between the city and the sea, a most difficult operation and one dismissed by the French as completely impracticable. The plan was to take a bridgehead by a *coup de main* with a small body of guards and then form a pontoon bridge from boats brought round to the mouth of the river by sea.

The first part of the operation went well and several hundred men were soon established on the north bank of the river. The French, few in number and completely surprised, were not able to break into the bridgehead but the pontoon boats ran into considerable difficulty, as the mouth of the river was made dangerous by stormy weather, and the safe passage past the bar was made almost impossible by the rough seas. However, one by one, the boats forced their way through, some being wrecked, but most passing safely to the bridgehead where a makeshift pontoon bridge was soon established. The rest of Hope's Corps now passed over with supporting troops.

Meanwhile the old crossing at Cambo was exploited by Hill

and Soult found himself forced away from the city of Bayonne, his main strongpoint. Leaving a garrison to hold the city he withdrew away north-east towards Toulouse closely followed by the British troops, and the British army, except for the men left to invest Bayonne, moved once again out of the Basque country.

X

THE BÉARN—A MOUNTAIN DUKEDOM

LYING hard by the eastern boundaries of the country of the Basques is the beginning of the real high Pyrenees; this is the mountain land of Béarn, the largest of the old Pyrenean states. Two great valleys run down from the high mountains to the plain below and around them are centred most of the life of Béarn. Two main water courses, the Gaves of Oloron and Pau, flow at an angle across the plain, and here is the richest agriculture with vines, orchards and cattle raising the main occupations. Béarn was first recorded as far back as 820, but in 841 the capital, Lescar, was destroyed by the Moors. A new capital, Morlaas, was built and the region became a Viscounty, a status that it maintained through many difficult years under the rule of the English, the Kings of Navarre and the Kings of France. Their independence was guaranteed by the Laws of Morlaas, which restricted the power of the Viscount, who had to swear to abide by the ancient declaration. In the year 1290 changes were to come, for Béarn became linked to the County of Foix, its near neighbour in the Pyrenees and the Counts of Foix became the Viscounts of Béarn.

One of the most notorious of the Counts and Viscounts was Gaston Phoebus. A great soldier and clever politician and a remarkable personality, he spent most of his life in amassing quantities of gold. He attacked his neighbours and demanded payments to keep the peace. He was paid four hundred thousand florins to leave the Languedoc in peace; two hundred thousand to restore the towns and cities that he had stormed, half a million florins ransom for Jean I of the province of Armagnac, who was taken with his knights at the battle of Launac, after Jean had been captured single-handed by Gaston himself. In 1376 he made peace with Jean II of Armagnac and agreed to the marriage of his only son with Beatrix, the daughter of Jean. However, the poor son did not live long to enjoy the delights of married life, for he was killed by his father after a domestic quarrel, when he was accused of trying to poison his father. Gaston kept up his remarkable career until he was sixty years old when on the way back from bear hunting he died of a stroke.

As Gaston died without an heir, his lands passed on to the family of Albrets who ruled through the seventeenth century. In 1527 Henri d'Albret married Marguerite d'Angoulême, a sister of Francis I. Marguerite was to be a great influence and became a leading intellectual and writer. Her works include a collection of love stories called the Heptameron. Her daughter Jeanne d'Albret married Antoine de Bourbon and their child Henry was to be the future Henry IV. She became Queen of Navarre on the death of her father, for the Salic law did not apply in the Pyrenean states. However, she was to cause periods of great upheaval by changing her religion from Catholic to Protestant. Royalist troops under Montluc drove out her supporters from Navarre and she was forced to flee to La Rochelle. Her son Henry of Navarre, brought up simply, was politically astute enough to change his religion several times before finally embracing Catholicism when he took the crown of France.

Béarn now became part of France, although, it was not officially annexed until 1620. It still retained many of its rights and privileges and its own Parliament, which met at Pau.

As we have seen, the people of Béarn live for the most part by agriculture, wine cultivation being well developed. The Juraçon is one of the best known with its gold colour. It is grown near Pau on chalk hills. Another wine is the Béarn Rosé, which is one of the oldest wines of the region, having been exported to Holland and Germany as far back as the seventeenth century.

The mountains are the source of pasture for the thousands of sheep and cattle that can be found in this region. Every year the great flocks move out of the lower valleys where they have spent the winter and commence the long ascent of the valleys, either the Aspe or the Ossau. Their shepherds and herdsmen move with them carrying their belongings on a donkey. As the weather improves and summer comes so they move further and further up the mountain to the very edge of the bare rock itself. Here the grass grows strongly in the short summer and the herdsmen use the milk to produce cheeses, sending them down to the lower valleys when they have prepared a good stock. Some herdsmen live in simple huts others in more substantial stone built cottages. Once they used to carry with them a huge wooden box which they filled with hay and into which they crept on the cold nights of spring and autumn. Like the Basques the solitary life seems to suit the men here but they are still happy to talk to the occasional visitor when he walks or climbs his way to them. In October or late September, as the days shorten so they start to make their way slowly back down the slope to escape the cold and the mists.

In the lower valleys, in addition to the pastoral life, there are a number of other local industries. Fine textiles are produced, especially table linens and blankets. Here, too, the famous berets so loved of the Basques and the people of Béarn are made. Special wooden hammers pound loose material into the well-known felt cloth which is then shaped to size. The local pigs are famous for their quality and it is here rather than in Bayonne, that now are produced most of the famous Bayonne hams. They are so called because the salt used in their curing comes from that city.

The two main valleys that reach up into the mountains from the plain of Béarn are those of the Aspe and Ossau. The Vallé d'Aspe follows the line of the gave or mountain torrent that rushes or sometimes literally falls down its length. At the head of the valley is the town of Oloron Ste Marie standing where the Gave d'Aspe and d'Ossau meet to form the Gave d'Oloron. Formerly one of the Roman cities of their route to Spain, it became a bishopric in the fourth century. However, the invasion of the Barbarians in the sixth century and the Moors in the eighth century completely destroyed the old city. In 1080 the Viscount of Béarn rebuilt the town on a new site at the same time the Bishops built up the original city, so that for a time two towns stood separated only by a fast running gave. The old castle of the Viscounts of Béarn, that stood here, has virtually disappeared, only a tower remaining. There are however two romanesque churches which are amongst the finest in all this region. The Sainte Croix was started in 1070, for a time it was taken over by the Protestants, but was returned to Catholicism in 1621. It had suffered badly and in later years attempts have been made to restore it, with somewhat mixed results. The porch dates from the nineteenth century but a small door on the North side is, in fact, Romanesque. Inside, the main feature is the huge cupola shaped like an eight pointed star. The church of Ste Marie, the former cathedral, was built in 1102, was destroyed by fire in the early part of the thirteenth century, rebuilt, damaged by lightning, repaired, but it than fell into the hands of the Protestants who used it as a stable. Later, like Ste Croix it was returned to

Catholicism and was extensively restored. It is famous for the doorway and for its magnificent tympanum, showing the Descent from the Cross.

Oloron remains a quiet country town with a rather grey look. Here are produced the local textiles, the sandals favoured by the inhabitants, the berets and, rather strangely, chocolate.

Soon after leaving Oloron the valley widens and is full of fields of maize and corn. At Escot, the mountains move in upon the valley with the Pic Roumendares reaching some five thousand feet in height. A little further is the town of Sarrance, where it is believed that Marguerite de Valois wrote part of the Heptameron. Also of interest is the rebuilt Convent and the church with a strange bell tower. Leaving Sarrance the valley closes in once again at Bedous. The village itself stands in a relatively open basin with fine views of the surrounding mountains. It is also a good centre for exploring the main peaks of this area. A narrow winding road leads up to the village which has a spectacular setting dominated by the Billare mountain.

Moving on over the Pont d'Enfer, the valley turns sharply to the Fort du Portalet, used quite recently as a prison for political detainees. A long staircase with some five hundred and six steps leads up to the fort. The road climbs up towards the frontier at the Col du Somport through fine woods of beech, where some of the few remaining bears of the Pyrenees are reliably reported to still live.

Running parallel to the valley of the Aspe a few miles to the east is the Valleé d'Ossau. Here again the Gave d'Ossau follows the valley down to the town of Oloron. As in the Vallée d'Aspe at first the valley is wide near to Oloron and as the foothills of the Pyrenees rise up they become covered with trees. The expanse of the Bois du Bager runs along the edge of the mountains proper. The first village is Arudy set in a bend in the Gave. There is a small church of the fifteenth century with some interesting sculptures and paintings. Similarly the next village, Louvie-Juzon, has a well-decorated church of the fifteenth

century; here the pulpit is made of finely carved wood. The tiny village of Castet overlooks the valley from a promontory above the man-made lake. Nearby are the ruins of the Château Gelos which dates from the thirteenth century.

A little further up the valley is the town of Bielle once the capital of the region of Ossau, full of charming old houses dating from the fifteenth and sixteenth centuries. The church of St Vivien of the fifteenth century has a flamboyant doorway, while in the sacristy is a chest in which is preserved a document recording all the ancient rights of the inhabitants of Ossau.

The main town of the valley is Laruns which has an attractive main square with an arcaded town hall. In front of the eighteenth century church is a bust representing a local man, who became a Hussar, and in the Battle of Sanfeld on 10th October 1806 killed Prince Louis de Prusse, nephew of Frederick of Prussia. In many ways more interesting than Laruns is the village of Beost, which is full of old houses. It has a church of the twelfth century with a beautiful romanesque doorway. Not far away is the quarry where the marble was excavated for the statues of the Place de la Concorde and the church of the Madeleine in Paris.

The road now starts the climb up into high mountains and eventually the Col du Portalet. The mountains now begin to make their presence felt closing in upon the valley in the gorge of Hourat. The Gave pours down in a series of waterfalls and water slides while the sides of the gorge rise steeply up towards the lofty peaks. Set in this long gorge is the spa town of les Eaux Chaudes, which has the usual slightly depressing air of the old thermal towns of the region. As usual too its seven different sources offer a wide range of cures including a treatment for those suffering from sterility.

Here, again, as in the Vallée d'Aspe is a Pont d'Enfer leading the road across the Gave and past one of the important power stations which form a chain down the valley. Reaching the small village of Gabas there is a chapel, just off the road, dating from 1121 when it was founded by Gaston IV, Viscount of Béarn, as part of the Hospice that once stood here to shelter the pilgrims on their way by one of the less popular routes to Spain and the tomb of St James at Compostella.

Gabas is a centre for exploring the high mountains that surround it, although there are only a few hotels and even fewer shops and facilities, stretched out along the main narrow street. The National Park of the Pyrenees has now done something to bring more people to this part of the valley for the most attractive parts of the park are within easy distance. The most impressive mountain of this part of the Pyrenees, if not the whole range, is the Pic du Midi d'Ossau with its narrow pointed bare rock peak nearly always either in or just protruding from a small cloud. To climb the mountain is not too difficult, but it needs a competent guide and takes between ten and eleven hours. The views from the top are breathtaking, from the Atlantic Ocean to the west to the long range of crests which is the main range of the Pyrenees stretching away towards the Mediterranean. The National Park is situated around the Pic and here can be seen those animals, who have lived in the mountain for thousands of years still timid and watchful, ready to disappear up into the distant inaccessible crags. The best known are the small brown-gold coloured isards or chamois who defy gravity with every leap and perch bird-like on needle-sharp rocks with thousands of feet of space falling away beneath them.

Above Gabas the road passes the impressive Barrage de Fabrèges holding back a vast area of water used to drive the power stations of the lower valley. The road runs alongside the lake then winds through the Pont de Camps and has a magnificent view of the Pic du Midi on the right hand side. The valley climbs steeply through the Défilé de Tournon before breaking out suddenly into a wide expanse of grassy slopes, giving long views of the surrounding mountains. Here are numerous sheep and cattle enjoying the summer growths of the rich pastures. The road winds up across this pleasant area to the actual Col, which is marked by a few indistinguished buildings, which fail to detract from the grandeur of the surroundings, for now in front the road falls away towards Aragon and the mountains of the Spanish side. From the Vallée d'Ossau is one of the few lateral passes in the Pyrenees, which runs from Laruns to Argelès-Gazost in the Bigorre region.

The climb is stiff at first as the road rises towards the spa of les Eaux Bonnes. For many years this has been one of France's most popular watering places. Standing at the entrance of the Gorge of the river Sourde it is sheltered, yet with an open aspect, with vast beech woods sweeping away to the south while the Montagne Verte guards the town on the north. The cures offered here are varied and it is claimed that the soldiers from Béarn who were wounded in the Battle of Pavia in 1552 came here to be cured and to recuperate. It is even claimed that it can lift depression from those who are weighed down by troubles. The town itself has a cheerful aspect and the summer sunshine may perhaps do as much to lift depression as any waters. It is also a centre for numerous excursions into the mountains including the menacing Pic du Ger which stands some eight thousand feet high.

Above les Eaux Bonnes the road runs through some charming green open countryside along the course of the river Valentin, climbing up in a series of hairpin bends towards Gourette. This resort is a relatively new development being almost entirely devoted to winter sports with a whole series of ski lifts, cable cars, small hotels and all the paraphernalia of the station de ski.

The road continues to climb steeply through the seemingly never ending beech woods to the Crête Blanche which gives some fine views over the high mountains notably of the Pic du Ger. The countryside here opens out into pastureland before reaching the top of the Col d'Aubisque. The road now runs into what must be one of the most spectacular parts of the whole of the Pyrenees. Cut into the side of the mountain the narrow roadway winds around every bump and indentation in the mountain face.

This is no place for nervous drivers. Yet the overall impression is one of the great strength of the mountains standing overlooking the plain of Béarn, stretching away as far as the eye can see hundreds of feet below. The Col du Soulor now leads down to the town of Arrens, another centre for excursions into the surrounding mountains. It has a church dating back to the fifteenth century and it stands in a picturesque setting. It has a fine porch and a window which was made somewhere around 1500. Nearby is the chapel of Pouey Laun which has some outstanding wood carving in the classical style. The whole area is dominated by the mountain Balaitous rising nearly ten thousand feet high. The climb to the top is a long although not too difficult operation but a guide is needed. The road now winds down in rather more gentle fashion to Aucun, where there is a romanesque church dating back to the eleventh century with a charming doorway with two marble pillars. The interior is also worth a visit, being largely romanesque although the altar is seventeenth century. The road now leaves the mountains proper and descends towards the lower valley and the next province, that of Bigorre.

Before leaving the Béarn we must look at the town that has dominated this whole region for centuries, Pau. Originally a small fort controlling a crossing point of the Gave, Pau grew slowly until Gaston Phoebus fortified it and extended the walls. In 1464 Pau became the capital of Béarn although still a small town, so small, in fact, that when the local Parliament met there was never enough accommodation for all the members. After the marriage of Henry D'Albret and Margaret of Angoulême she spent much time restoring and redecorating the castle. On the 13th December 1553, the daughter of Margaret gave birth to a son here, the future Henry IV of France. So that her son should be born in Bèarn, she travelled by coach for nineteen days from Picardy. Traditionally the baby was given some wine from the Bèarn vineyard of the Clos de Gaye. During his boyhood his mother's conversion to Protestantism brought a puritanical reaction and the brilliant entertainments of the earlier period were abandoned.

Later, after Henry had become King of France and Navarre, Béarn became part of France and in 1620 King Louis XIII ceremonially entered Pau. Although still a relatively small town Pau now began to grow, monasteries were founded, also a university.

The British influence in Pau had always been strong and when in 1814 after the fall of Toulouse and Bayonne, a British army was based on Pau its popularity grew rapidly. Many of the British officers returned to settle and enjoy the climate, so much so that by 1863, of the total population of some twenty thousand, about three thousand were British. As is usual when they live abroad the British brought with them their own customs. Perhaps the most interesting and incongruous of these as far as Pau is concerned was the importance of fox hunting. Even today a regular fox hunt meets on the outskirts of Pau. The kennels are situated on the road near Morlaas.

The town itself is now modern and bustling, but it still has a feeling of history and above all of being a town that belongs to the mountains. It only needs a few minutes on the Boulevard des Pyrénées, a remarkable platform built on the very edge of the valley, looking out south towards the range of the Pyrenees, to appreciate this link. From this viewpoint some sixty miles length of the range can be seen with the high peaks always covered with snow.

At the very beginning of the Boulevard is the Château set in a naturally strong position on a promontory guarded on one side by the Gave and on the other by a steep ravine. The oldest parts of the castle date back to the thirteenth century. In 1370 Gaston Phoebus, using stone from the hillside, built the three walls and the central keep. In later years the defensive nature of the building changed as it was needed as a residence. Henry IV on becoming King, however, lost interest in the castle and moved much of the furniture to other royal *châteaux*. The castle now fell into disrepair and for nearly two hundred years was completely neglected. It was not until the time of the Second Empire and the rule of Napoleon III and the earlier rule of Louis Philippe, that anything was done to restore the building. The top of the keep, the windows, part of the south wing and the north wing were made good and now the château is worth a visit. Outstanding is the Grand Staircase first installed in 1528 and restored in 1869. There are some very fine Gobelins and Flemish tapestries. In the southern wing is the Béarn museum which is full of details of the life of this region.

A few miles to the north of Pau is the historic city of Lescar. Founded originally by the Romans as *Beneharnum* from which the name Béarn originally came, it was destroyed in 850 by the Moors. Later in 980 it was rebuilt but only a slightly different site as Lescarris. Today its great attraction is its former cathedral; a fine romanesque building dating from the twelfth century, it is over one hundred and eighty feet long. It was restored at the end of the fourteenth century and again several times in later years, it has however preserved in large measure its original style. Particularly fine is the main door while inside, the vaulting is extremely elegant for the romanesque building of these years. Here are buried some twelve members of the royal family of Navarre and recent excavations brought to light bones dating back to the fifteenth and sixteenth centuries. These bones were presumed to have been those of Margaret of Navarre, Jean D'Albret and Henry II of Navarre.

On the south side of the church is a side terrace sheltered by a large cedar, from here there are some breathtaking views across the mountains of the Pyrenees, reaching up from the far-distant horizon. Nearby are some remains of the old walls and fortifications and the remains of a strongpoint the Fort de l'Esquirette of the fourteenth century. The gateway leads down to the lower town and the old Couvent de Barnabites.

The small town that replaced Beneharnum as capital of Béarn after its destruction was Morlaas which is also but a short distance from Pau. Here again it is only its church which retains its importance. Founded in 1089 the main door is another good example of the local romanesque although it has been extensively restored.

Further north again is the town that replaced Morlaas as the third capital of Béarn, Orthez. Originally part of the region of Dax, Orthez was acquired by the Viscounts of Béarn in

the twelfth century. It became the favourite residence of the Viscounts and became a centre of the Reformed Church and the Protestant faith. In turn it was recaptured by Catholic forces and then by the Protestants under their outstanding leader, Montgomery, who promptly ravaged the whole town. This attack was followed by an outbreak of the plague, which caused even more suffering.

It was here, too, that the advancing army of Wellington arrived in February 1814 after forcing the French under Soult away from their strong positions near Bayonne. Soult's army now reduced to some thirty thousand men was established on the hills to the north and north west of the town. Once again Wellington attacked strongly and despite yet another brave stand the French were forced back away from the strong position and withdrew along the road towards Toulouse. General Foy, one of the outstanding commanders on the French side received his fortieth wound in this engagement and a memorial stands on this spot. The town today is a quiet country place well-known for its Bayonne hams and its market for pigs, calves, chickens and *foie gras*. In the centre of the town is the Pont Vieux which dates from the thirteenth century. It has four fine arches and a tower for its defence, built in the middle of the bridge. Also worth a visit is the Tour Moncade which stands on a grassy promontory overlooking the town. It is all that remains of the castle built by Gaston VII in 1242. The castle was the scene of some of the remarkable feasts and rich distractions organised by Gaston Phoebus during his reign. Some of these events are recounted by the famous French chronicler, Froissart, in his writings.

The Viscounts of Béarn had links with another town in this area, Sauveterre de Béarn. The story goes that the widow of Gaston V of Béarn was accused of killing her baby, born after the death of her husband. Her brother Sanche, King of Navarre ordered her to be submitted to the judgement of God. Her hands and feet were tied and she was thrown from the old bridge, of which part still stands, into the raging Gave. The waters, however, bore her gently to the bank where she was washed up unharmed. Being proved innocent she was restored to her position and privileges. The view from the ruins of the old bridge is well worth the walk down. The town has also preserved part of its original fortifications and the remains of the castle and keep of Montréal built in the twelfth century with a large central bell tower and a beautifully executed doorway.

South along the Gave d'Oloron is the quaint old town of Navarrenx. Originally on the left bank of the Gave the town was rebuilt and fortified by the King of Navarre, Henri d'Albret in 1546 according to plans drawn up by the Sicilian architect

Fabrici Siciliano. The fortifications were reinforced by Vauban after the town fell to Louis XIII. They are very well kept and included strongpoints, look-out towers and other defences. Across the Gave on the old site of the town is the Tour Herrere dating from the fifteenth century.

Nowadays the main interest in Navarrenx is in fishing, particularly salmon fishing and every year what are somewhat impressively called the Salmon Fishing World Championships are held here.

South of Pau along the Gave are a whole series of small villages, perhaps the most interesting of these is Nay on the left bank of the Gave. It is now a centre for making the popular berets both for the local people and for the Basques themselves. The town hall is a charmingly arcaded structure while in the square is the house of Jeanne D'Albret in the style of the Renaissance town house. The church is Gothic of the fifteenth century with some well carved wooden decoration. Every year on the third Tuesday after All Saints' Day is a great horse fair. The winding road leads on to Coarraze where the future Henry IV was brought up as a child. He was left to live the life of a simple peasant of Béarn in the country château so that he should always remember that he was of these people. Just after the small village of Lestelle Bétharram is the Sanctuary de Notre Dame de Bétharram, which is the object of an important pilgrimage every year in the second week of September. It was originally built as a thanksgiving after a young girl who was drowning in the Gave appealed to the Virgin Mary for help. At that moment an oar was washed into her hand and with its aid she was able to struggle ashore.

The road now crosses the Gave by the old bridge of Bétharram built in 1687, it has a fine sturdy arch and is covered with ivy giving it an even more ancient appearance. Just off the road here are the fascinating Grottes de Bétharram. These caves were discovered only in the eighteenth century and were arranged for public visits in 1903. There are five galleries running for over three miles. Access from the car park is by an interesting aerial train called a Télévoiture which travels some nine feet off the ground. The caves have some weird stalactites and stalagmites. From here the road swings away to the east across the face of the high mountains towards the centre of the Pyrenean range and the region of Bigorre.

XI

THE BIGORRE—LOURDES AND A MODERN PILGRIMAGE

TODAY the Department of the Hautes Pyrénées corresponds almost exactly to the old Province of Bigorre, and here, in truth, are the Pyrenees reaching up to their highest point that also marks the frontier. Here are the great peaks of the Vignemale, nearly eleven thousand feet high and the Balaitous over ten thousand feet, not forgetting the impressive Pic du Midi-de-Bigorre. This is the dramatic and beautiful area full of stark bare rocks interspersed with charming sheltered valleys, clear still lakes, bustling mountain torrents and, of course, the spectacular cirques or natural basins of which the best known are at Gavarnie and Troumouse.

The mountain area or the Lavedan, as it is known, is full of passes between the high crests but none are easy, whether they lead from east to west along the line of the ridge or north to south through the main massif. Some can be used by motor-car and others only by mule or on foot. The Col du Tourmalet, which leads up to the Pic du Midi has a road which rises to some eight thousand six hundred feet, the highest in the Pyrenees and the second highest in all France. Seven main valleys lead into the mountains from the plain below, four on the left bank of the Gave de Pau, Saint Savin, l'Extreme Salles, Batsuguères and Azu. In the centre is the main valley, that of Barèges, while two further valleys, Castelloubon and Davantaygue join the right bank of the Gave. These seven valleys or Parsan as they are called are still somewhat remote and in former times they enjoyed a large measure of autonomy. The foothills of the mountains here run out quickly into the plain where the Gave de Pau, soon to become the Adour, and the Nests d'Aure soon to become the Garonne, turn into real rivers. Here are the larger and the more prosperous areas around Lourdes and Tarbes. Further north again are the bare plateaux of Ger and Lannemezan.

The area was first mentioned in Roman times, *Tarba ubi castrum Bigorra* says Caesar in his Commentaries. But it was not until the ninth century that it became a county with its main centre at Tarbes. In 1097 it is recorded that the overlord Bernard II confirmed that the rights and privileges of these independently minded people by agreeing to a document that stated that he could be their lord for as long as he respected these ancient rights, if he failed to do so he would no longer be recognised. The democratic spirit of these mountain people has been in evidence ever since. As we have seen, Salic law preventing female inheritance did not apply in the Pyrenees, so that the County of Bigorre had a series of Countesses some being of formidable character.

In the early part of the thirteenth century the English came to Bigorre and after a series of revolts and bloody campaigns and bitter retributions the English were finally forced out in 1406. The mountaineers of the Lavedan played a large part in this struggle to maintain their own rule. Every new Count of Bigorre had to go to the people of the Lavedan to confirm this rule and to accept their affirmation of loyalty. However, it seems to have been a somewhat risky undertaking, for invariably, hostages were taken and held in the castle at Lourdes until the safe return of the Count. In later years these people were to cause considerable difficulty to the representatives of the crown and especially to anyone who had ideas of such strange things as tax collecting. Near Argelès is a precipice known as the Saut-du-Procureur where by tradition an over enthusiastic tax collector met his doom at the hands of a band of local people. The salt tax which caused difficulty in less militant areas caused a complete revolt here with some seven thousand men under arms. The salt tax never was collected.

The people of Bigorre live for the most part by agriculture. Cattle and sheep that can live in the valleys or on the mountain pastures climbing easily and seemingly completely unattended. Lower down on the plain maize is the staple crop and inevitably the geese and poultry that form such a large part of the local gastronomic specialities.

There are some small industrial developments near Tarbes and Bagnères-de-Bigorre while the great marble quarries at Campan and Sarrancolin are still producing high grade marble after nearly three hundred years of working. Tourism has now become of major importance growing out of the original visitors who came to be cured at the many spas and thermal establishments. There are pilgrims too, not the dull grey clothed figures who once made their way across the mountains to Santiago, but modern, ordinary people from all classes, rich and poor, from many races but all devout in their Catholicism who come year after year seeking a miracle at the shrine at Lourdes.

In 1844 the miller of Lourdes had a daughter Bernadette. The family were poor and Bernadette had five other brothers and sisters. Bernadette, the eldest, was very delicate and had that slightly ethereal air that this type of child sometimes develops. She lived away from the family home with a nurse at Bartres where she tended sheep. Early in 1858 she returned home to be prepared for her first communion and she studied at the school attached to the Hospice of Lourdes. On a holiday from school she was out collecting wood near the Grotto of

Massabielle, she entered the Grotto and had a vision of the Virgin Mary.

Eighteen times she was to have this vision in this place and many people were to come to see the supposed miracle. On the occasion of her ninth vision Bernadette bent down and dug up the ground with her hands, at once a spring appeared where before no water had ever flowed. This was the miracle of the spring and its reputation for curing the sick was soon to spread. A great church was built nearby. Bernadette was examined about her visions by the ecclesiastical authorities and after every possible check they were declared genuine, and in 1862 the devotions at this place were authorised. Bernadette became a nun at the Convent of St Gildard at Lourdes, where she became Sister Marie Bernard, but she died in 1879 when she was just thirty-five years old. She was made a saint in 1933 by which time Lourdes had become the second greatest place of pilgrimage after Rome for Catholics. The numbers of pilgrims coming to Lourdes annually exceed three million and the great feature of this pilgrimage is the special attention paid to the sick. Here they come in search of a miracle. Often declared incurable or hopeless cripples this is perhaps the last hope, the last possible effort. Thus Lourdes is for many a sad place; it is sad to see the long lines of cripples waiting in their wheel chairs, patiently more than pathetically to move forward in the great processions; it is sad to see them arrive in the city, often from far off lands; it is sad to see them leave, often as they came and as they are to remain.

What of the miraculous cures so often claimed? These are investigated in detail by a special medical commission before any judgement is given. Some cures are so approved, but what they represent in numbers or even percentages of the numbers who come is difficult to say. But maybe the great emotional experience that many undergo does in fact play a part in their recovery or at least in helping them to a new mental outlook. But it is not easy to forget the tawdry shops selling the cheap plastic bottles for the pilgrims to collect and take away their holy water, the incongruous commercialisation of the faith is so close to the more mundane needs of man.

The Basilica du Rosaire was constructed in front of the Grotto in 1889. It stands dominating the whole scene in a wide semi-circle overlooking the long winding lines of pilgrims making their way up to and from the Grotto. The church itself is built in a strange Byzantine style, which makes it look as if it got here by some weird mistake of history.

It looks across the river towards the old town of Lourdes set amongst green fields and woods, not at all the setting one would expect for the elaborate architecture of the present building. In 1958 it became necessary to improve the accommodation for the pilgrims and a second Basilica was built, this time underground. This is the Basilica of St Pius X. Here twenty thousand people can be accommodated, making it the second largest church in the world after St Peter's in Rome. It is spanned by ribs of pre-stressed concrete attached to central supports, the outer arms taking the thrust of the side aisles. This means that there are no intermediate supporting columns and that the vast crowds of pilgrims can move easily inside.

Yet it is only in recent times that Lourdes has found fame and fortune as a religious centre; before that it had been one of the principal towns of Bigorre for hundreds of years. At first, it was a small fortified place on the hill overlooking the river in the times of the Roman occupation. Later it fell into the hands of the Moors who held it against all attacks. Charlemagne himself attempted to recapture it but was forced to organise a long siege. The Moors suffered badly from lack of food when one day they were about to surrender, a bird dropped a fish into the castle. The leader of the Moors decided to send the fish to Charlemagne so that he would be disheartened about the success of the siege. Charlemagne was about to order his troops to withdraw, when the Bishop of Le Puy is said to have had a dream, that he should suggest to the Moors that they should surrender not to Charlemagne but to the church of Notre Dame de Puy. The Moors accepted, for this meant their lives would be spared, and their leader became a Christian taking the name of Lorus from which the name Lourdes was in turn to come.

The Château de Lourdes stands up high on this very spot overlooking the present town. It is a fine example of a mediaeval castle although the access to it by a strange rickety lift up the outside face of the main tower hardly adds to this impression. There are over one thousand yards of fortifications, a drawbridge and a fourteenth century keep, all to some extent restored. The castle became the property of the town in 1894 and it now houses an excellent museum of the Pyrenees. A beautifully conceived pattern of exhibits laid out to give the maximum effect give a clear idea of life as it is and as it has been in these mountains. Most exhibits come from the Béarn and the Basque areas. The elaborate and yet simple costumes of the regions are all shown here and the process of life, as it was really lived in the home, in the fields and in the mountains. There is also a library containing some fourteen thousand books and documents on the Pyrenees.

North of Lourdes is the other large town of Bigorre and the gateway to the region from France, Tarbes. Now a pleasant bustling town, an important route centre, a market place, Tarbes has a history of disaster and bloodshed that it is hard to equal even in this often ravaged part of France.

As we have seen, Tarbes was already a provincial centre when the Romans came and it developed under their rule. In the tenth century it was fortified by Raymond I and became capital of the County of Bigorre. It was seized and occupied by the English from 1360 to 1406. In 1569 it was stormed by the Protestant army under Montgomery who drove out the population, burnt the churches and the convents. Gradually the inhabitants made their way back, but no sooner had they started the task of rebuilding, when the Viscount de Montamat, one of the lieutenants of Montgomery, attacked the town a second time, levelling the walls and fortifications he left it in ruins and undefended. In 1592 it was attacked again by troops from Comminges who devastated the surrounding countryside until they were finally driven out in 1595. But there was still one more campaign to come; as Wellington's rapidly advancing columns reached Tarbes in 1814, a French force attempted to make a stand under the walls of the town but once again without success and after a sharp fight they withdrew along the road to Toulouse.

Tarbes has always been known as a horse breeding centre, and it was claimed that the finest cavalry horses came from its Haras or stud founded in 1806. In the Museum Massey a whole section is devoted to the cavalry horse of Tarbes, which is believed to be a cross between local strains and Moorish and even English stock. The museum also covers the history of the regiments of Hussars that were equipped with the local horses.

Also interesting is the Cathedral of Notre Dame-de-la-Sède a romanesque structure built on the benedictine plan, but extensively restored in later years. The font which dates from the thirteenth century was used in the baptism of a local child, who was to grow up to be Marshal Foch, first Allied Supreme Commander. The house where he was born can be seen appropriately in the Rue de la Victoire.

From Lourdes the roads run south towards the Lavedan. The main route follows the Gave de Pau along a narrow winding valley past the village of Vidalos where the keep of a castle built by the Counts of Bigorre in 1175 still stands. Soon however, the valley widens out into a pleasant green spacious plain. Here is one of the most popular resorts of the area, Argelès-Gazost. An old established thermal establishment has been used as the basis of developing the town as a general tourist centre with some delightful excursions into the nearby mountains. There is a sharp difference between the resort and the old town which stands on a small hill.

On leaving Argelès it is best to follow the old road to St Savin, one of the outstanding religious centres of this region. The Roman governors of Bigorre had a residence here which was later used by a Christian priest and his disciples as a base for their missionary work. Charlemagne himself assisted them to build an abbey. In 843 the Vikings burned the abbey to the ground, but it was rebuilt in 945 by Raymond I who also presented the abbey with the land in the valley of Cauterets. Thus St Savin became both a religious and administrative centre.

Today only the abbey church remains, originally built in the twelfth century it was fortified in the fourteenth century and the footway used by the guards still remains. There is a fine romanesque door but the church is best known for its decoration including a wooden carved figure of Christ of outstanding beauty. On the left of the choir are two large paintings on wood dating from the fifteenth century. Each is divided into nine sections and tell the story of the life of St Savin. Outside the church the main square is full of old houses and has a stone cross dating from 1783. Not far away is the ruined castle of Arcinas Avant, built by the Black Prince and dating from the end of the fourteenth century. The road leads on through quiet pleasant countryside to the larger town of Pierrefitte where the Gave de Cauterets flows into the Gave de Pau. Now mainly a route centre, Pierrefitte is another well-equipped resort for mountain excursions. Not far away at Beaucens are some interesting old ruins, including a twelfth century keep and a castle with a double line of fortifications which was once the favourite residence of the Viscounts of Lavedan.

Once into the valley of Cauterets the roads begin to climb steeply through woods of chestnut trees. The valley closes in and the scene becomes more and more familiar, bare rock and steep crags of the high mountains. Cauterets itself is one of the most important resorts of the Pyrenees. Important as a spa, a summer excursion centre and a winter sports resort it has much to offer. When Raymond I presented the valley to the Abbey of St Savin, he instructed that they should build a church and some baths on this spot.

This was done and by the sixteenth century the curative capabilities of the waters became famous after a visit of Margaret of Navarre, sister of François I, who came to be cured from rheumatism. Whilst here she continued with her writings and her Heptameron. The town took as its motto *A Cauterets, tout que gareix*, 'At Cauterets you can be cured of anything'. From Cauterets there is a wide range of walks, climbs and excursions of all kinds but perhaps one of the most spectacular is that to the Pont D'Espagne and the Lac de Gaube. The road up to the Pont D'Espagne is strictly controlled in summer with a one way system, only up in the early part of the afternoon and only down in the latter part. The road climbs steeply through a spectacular view with huge rocks and a succession of lofty waterfalls. The Lac de Gaube lies further on some six thousand feet high in a setting that even in the region of mountain peaks is as dramatic and breathtaking as could be imagined.

From Pierrefitte the Gave de Pau swings away south towards Luz St Sauveur. The gorge here is narrow, with just the rushing Gave and the road filling the available space. Luz is the former capital of the Valley of Barèges and lies in a wide part of the valley with small hills running down to the town itself. It has a gay holiday atmosphere probably due to the brightly painted hotels and cafés, which form its main industry. In the centre of the town is the famous church of the Templars, but in fact it never belonged to them, being rather the property of the Hospitaliers de St Jean, later to become the Knights of Malta. The church was built in the twelfth century and like St Savin it was fortified in the fourteenth century to provide a sanctuary for the local people.

Immediately adjacent is the spa of St Sauveur whose main claim to fame seems to have been a two months stay by Napoleon III. This resulted in an improvement in a number of local amenities notably the building of a splendid single arch bridge across the Gave, the Pont Napoleon. A marble column stands supporting an Imperial Eagle as a thanksgiving to the Emperor, who was responsible for its construction. The road follows the steep-sided valley up towards Gavarnie. Gradually the mountains seem to close in as the road winds, turning and twisting in its attempt to follow the tortuous Gave. Suddenly the mountains appear to step back and the whole of the splendid Cirque de Gavarnie appears in view.

Gavarnie itself is but a small village. At the entrance is a statue to Count Henry Russel, an eccentric mountaineer who did so much to open up the Pyrenees to climbers. An Irishman who was born and lived in France and who inherited a foreign title, he spent much of his time here and in the mountains. As far as the Vignemale was concerned, literally in it, for he dug out some caves in the side of the mountain so that he could live there when the fancy took him. In the village there are a few hotels and some houses belonging to the mountain guides or mountaineers. It is essentially an excursion centre but the main excursion it has to offer is one of the finest in all these mountains.

The Cirque de Gavarnie can be reached on foot from the village in about one hour but it seems as if everyone follows the old tradition and makes the journey either by horse or mule. The horses standing quietly in rows waiting for customers gives Gavarnie the air of a frontier town, whence the tourists are setting out on some far-flung expedition. Practically all, however, return safely a couple of hours later. The Cirque stands tall and imposing dominating everything around it. Waterfalls pour down the front of the bare rocks making strange white lines on the grey background. In the words of Victor Hugo 'It is both a mountain and a wall'. The base of the wall is some five thousand feet high and the peaks reach up to nearly ten thousand feet. A curious niche in the crest is locally known as the Brèche de Roland and can be reached on foot with some difficulty. A new motor road leads from the village up to the Col de Boucharo on the frontier but here it stops, for the road on the Spanish side is not yet started, let alone completed. From here it is easier to reach the Brèche de Roland although it must not be confused with the Fausse Brèche alongside it. Strangely enough the view of the back of the Cirque on the Spanish side is also dramatic, the river Ordesa flows through the Cañon d'Arrazas backed by great red-coloured cliffs that look almost like the Grand Canyon. Another Cirque, that of Troumouse, is more difficult to reach and is less spectacular than Gavernie but still has a remarkable quality.

From Luz another road climbs eastwards towards the Pic du Midi. The first town is Barèges, another thermal centre, which has in recent years developed its winter sports facilities. A long straggling village, it follows the road as it climbs steadily up the valley of the Bastan. The waters have a reputation for curing war wounds and for many years a military hospital has been established here. For skiers, there are two main lifts and also a funicular railway, which climbs six thousand feet up the Pic d'Ayré. There are some particularly interesting excursions from Barèges, including the so-called Montagne

Fleurie because of its great appeal to botanists, who come to study the wild flowers, that grow in profusion on its slopes. It is also possible to reach the Refuge Packe high up in the massif of the Néouville and named after the famous British mountaineer, who did so much to make climbing in this area as popular as the Alps. Packe was a scientist and a student of the classics. He was from Stretton Hall in Leicestershire, where he was the squire. His great work on the Pyrenees was a *Guide to the Pyrenees*, especially intended for mountaineers.

Above Barèges the valley winds slowly up through steep-sided meadows. From the right the valley of the Escoubous runs into the main valley and the road crosses the charming yet fast-flowing stream from this valley. A new road linking Barèges to the Valley of the Nest D'Aure to the south by a series of mountain lakes is planned. At present it is only possible to reach these lakes by foot or in jeeps and then on foot. Cold, still and clear these lakes looked as if they have been tucked into folds and cracks in the mountains, but they are full of fish and the trout come easily to the the line.

The Col du Tourmalet rises rapidly towards the Pic du Midi. A controlled road leads up from the Col to Les Laquets. Although it skirts round sheer drops and at places is no more than a ledge in the rock it is, in fact, safe. From Les Laquets a cable car leads up to the Observatory of the Pic. The Observatory can be visited and some of the detailed scientific observation work that takes place here seen. The size of the buildings and complexities of the studies that take place at this height are astonishing.

From the Col the road descends rapidly to La Mongie, a modern well-equipped ski resort with a delightful modern chapel. At the bottom of the long descent the road reaches the route and waterway centre of St Marie de Campan, a small market town and summer resort. From Ste Marie the road runs north through a succession of small villages along the valley of the Adour, and eventually to Bagnères-de-Bigorre.

It is yet another of the splendid little thermal spas of the region. Known too by the Romans as *Vicus Aquensis*, it has a history of visits by famous people right up to the present day. Nearby is the former Abbey of Escaladieu in a beautiful setting on the confluence of the Luz and the Arros. The original Cistercian Abbey was founded in 1136 some distance away, but was transferred here in 1142 and its Abbey church completed in 1160 is the oldest in France after the church at Fontenay in Burgundy. It is built on an identical plan. The Abbey was damaged by the Protestants during the wars of religion in 1567. The Abbey was restored and reoccupied in the seventeenth century but was sold during the Revolution. Only part of the church remains. A little further on up a steep road is the Château de Mauvezin of the thirteenth century. One of the most powerful strongholds of Gaston Phoebus, it stands on a promontory with a superb view looking out towards the Pyrenees. It has been extensively restored in the twentieth century.

From Ste Marie another road runs southwards towards the Col d'Aspin. One of the most attractive of the Pyrenean passes, with great forest of beech and oak and fir. The Col itself is very open with herds of cows wandering over its green pastures. The descent is rapid and the road winds steeply down to Arreau. In the main street is a finely preserved old house, the Maison Valencia Labat, of the sixteenth century, while on the right bank of the river is the Chapel of St Exupere with its romanesque doorway. Under the porch is a large bin once used for storing wheat and now used as a collection box for gifts.

From Arreau there is one of the finest mountain drives in the Pyrenees, along the valley of the Neste D'Aure. Once this valley like so many others was virtually self-governing although technically under the rule of the Kings of Aragon before passing under the rule of the Armagnac family and eventually the Kings of France in 1475. The road climbs slowly to Cadeac with its twelth century watch-tower to pass in front of the chapel of Notre Dame de Pene Taillade with its façade decorated in curious style by a sixteenth century frescoe.

St Lary, once a village, is now a rapidly developing winter sports centre with fine modern hotels, ski lifts and all the outward signs of the new style mountain architecture. Above St Lary is a narrow gorge with, high above, the village of Tramezaygues with the ruins of the castle that once guarded the valley. After the village of Fabian the road climbs up the steep face of the rock towards the Lac de Cap de Long. This is one of the most difficult roads in the Pyrenees narrowly winding upwards in a series of seemingly never ending hairpin bends until, suddenly, when it seems that the top will never come, the road leads out onto a ridge overlooking, far below, the Lac D'Oredon. Here is the largest of all the many dams in the Pyrenees, making the artificial Lac de Cap de Long set in the very heart of the mountains themselves. The Néouville massif reaches up all around the lake. It is near to the Lac D'Oredon at the foot of the cliff that the Route des Lacs from Barèges will eventually run.

From the town of Arreau it is also possible to continue on, towards the Col de Peyresourde wandering gently through a succession of villages. The climb to the Col is steep at first, then slightly easier as the crest is reached. Here again are the high pastures and the road descends through them passing the tiny romanesque chapel of St Pé de la Moraine on the way down to Cazaux de Larboust, where the romanesque church of the twelfth century is worth a visit to see the frescoes. From here there is another superb mountain excursion to the Lac d'Oo; en route can be seen some waterfalls, including one known as Magdalen's Hair because of the silvery streaks which hang like strands of hair across the rocks. The road soon reaches St Aventin, where there is a church of the ninth century with a romanesque doorway. The church is supposed to have been built on the spot where St Aventin, a hermit of the eighth century, died leaping from the rocks above to escape the Moors, who were pursuing him. The road has now reached almost half way along the range between the Atlantic and the Mediterranean and it is here that the mountains form yet another region of this varying landscape.

XII

THE ROMAN CITY OF ST BERTRAND DE COMMINGES

THE high mountains continue into the region of le Comminges, in fact the highest mountain in the Pyrenees, the Pic D'Aneto is part of its central massif although the actual mountain stands in Spain. But here as opposed to the Bigorre there are few practicable passes either across the frontier into Spain, or even east-west along the chain itself. For most of the time the frontier with Spain follows the highest point of the range, but here, for some reason, the line changes and the Val d'Aran and the source of one of France's great rivers, the Garonne, lie in Spain. It is only in recent years that access has been available from the Spanish side, when in 1948 a four mile long road tunnel was driven through under the Port de Viella. The road follows the valley of the Garonne into France at the Pont du Roi whence it flows quickly down to the plain growing rapidly as it is fed by the mountain torrents on the French side.

Le Comminges was one of the important Roman settlements and in this area there is a good deal of interesting remains of those ages. Later le Comminges became part of Aquitaine but in the tenth century it was incorporated into a part of the County of Toulouse and eventually became part of France in 1453.

Like the Bigorre this is a cattle-raising area but also of great importance are the vast forests of pine trees. Paper making has been long established and the University of Toulouse has a research station near Jueu. When Louis XIV decided to build up the French Navy much of the timber needed came from these forests. Around Luchon there are mostly pine woods, while beech grow at Arbas and Cagire and poplars along the Garonne valley. Tourism has had its influence here, too, and today many a once quiet mountain town and valley are now busy summer or winter resorts. Visitors come for many reasons, but one of the most important that brings them here are the treasures of the past, for le Comminges is particularly rich in these, and perhaps no town is richer than St Bertrand de Comminges.

The town is a gem of its kind, built on a small hill overlooking the Garonne valley, surrounded by walls and fortifications. Full of architectural and historical interest stretching back over two thousand years, St Bertrand is almost unique of its kind. The first town built here was in 72 B.C. by tribesmen from the southern side of the mountains who were driven northwards by the advancing power of Rome, in the form of Pompey and his armies. But soon the Romans were to come and settle here and the town grew and developed as *Lugdunum Convenarum*, and in A.D. 37 Herod Antipas, Tetrarch of Galilee, was exiled here by the Emperor Caligula. It drew wealth from its thermal waters and marble quarries always highly prized by the Romans and its population grew and prospered.

In 408, however, the Barbarian invasions reached the town and the lower town was captured and destroyed, the fortifications of the upper town on its small hill held out, but the Roman settlement was obliterated. The main town continued to survive many troubles and attacks until the sixth century when a certain Gondowald, who was attempting to establish a claim to rule over all central Gaul, was driven back upon the town by troops of Gontran, the King of Burgundy. Entering the town with a few of his followers, he was trapped by the Burgundians who laid siege. The inhabitants hoping to avoid this threat to their city seized Gondowald and threw him over the walls to the besiegers. The Burgundians, however, were not impressed and razed the town and killed or drove out the entire population.

For six centuries the town remained a heap of abandoned ruins until Bishop Bertrand de l'Isle-Jourdain decided that the site was an admirable one for the Cathedral he wanted to build. Work started early in the twelfth century and soon a small town grew up around the cathedral, which took its name from its founder, who was later canonised as St Bertrand. With the development of the great pilgrimages it became yet another stopping place on the way to Compostella and a meeting place for the thousands of pilgrims on that route to the south. Like St Jean Pied-de-Port it prospered greatly at this time catering for the pilgrim's every need, but soon the pilgrims were to travel no more and gradually the town became neglected; its prosperity waned and for hundreds of years it passed once more into semi-oblivion. The Revolution deposed its Bishop and it was finally left with its memories and its enormous historical heritage.

The main entrance to the town is by the Porte Cabirole, which bears a mutilated inscription dedicating the town to the Emperor Claudius and dating from A.D. 51 or 52. On either side of the gateway are two old houses probably from the sixteenth century. The one on the left was the house occupied by the bishops for many years. The road up to the Cathedral passes the Maison Bridault of 1420, recently restored and now occupied by the Post Office. The Cathedral itself is on the very top of the hill, and it is in two distinct parts. The first is the romanesque façade with its porch surmounted by a tympanum showing the Adoration of the Magi and the second the Apostles. Above the porch is a bell tower which was once fortified, with wooden galleries secured to the top. Inside the church the first two bays of the nave are romanesque but the rest of the church is Gothic. Now here is the contrast between the heavy solid romanesque style with its small windows, thick walls and dark interior and the light uplifted Gothic so clearly marked.

The church was originally built as an act of faith but the coming of the great pilgrimages brought a necessity for more space and in 1304 Bertrand-de-Goth, then Bishop of Bordeaux and one time Bishop of Comminges, decided to enlarge the existing church. The old building was largely demolished and the new Gothic section constructed. In 1535 the Bishop Jean-de-Mauleon was responsible for the famous woodwork which includes the rood screen, the choir screen, the bishop's throne and the choir stalls. On the sixty-six choir stalls are some remarkable carvings covering a wide range of subjects, some righteous and some very much less so. But it is perhaps something outside the church, that is the really superb feature of the cathedral. On the south side are the finest cloisters that have ever been built. On three sides the galleries are romanesque and on the north side alongside the Cathedral is a Gothic gallery. It is not in fact the size or elaborations that make these cloisters so impressive, but rather the simplicity allied with their situation looking out towards the mountains almost as if here is where men themselves have reached out after truth.

After this, all other visits in the town seem something of an anti-climax, but worth a detour are the two museums, where some of the remains of the Roman city which once stood at the foot of the hill now are housed. In the Galerie du Trophé are some statues all to some extent damaged while at the

Museum of Comminges there is a wider range of material. The actual Roman settlement has now been extensively excavated and amongst the places discovered are the Forum, thermal baths, a theatre and an amphitheatre. Nearby in a quiet somewhat isolated spot is the charming little church of St Just, built in the eleventh and twelfth centuries. There is a fine Romanesque gate leading into the churchyard with a Roman funeral plaque just on its right.

A short distance further on is the town of St Gaudens, named after a thirteen year old martyr slaughtered by the Barbarians in 475. On the main square stands the church of St Pierre and St Gaudens, a former collegiate church in the Romanesque style of the eleventh century. It can, however, still give us a good idea of how the original romanesque church at St. Bertrand de Comminges looked, for it is built on an identical plan. Saint Gaudens, a small rather dusty town useful only as a centre for visits to the surrounding villages, is now coming out of its slumber, for here natural gas has been found opening up a vast prospect of new industries and new life.

Some miles to the east along the valley of the Salat is the pleasant town of St Girons, which stands on the confluence of Salat, the Lez and the Baup. Apart from being a tourist resort it is also a centre of the paper-making manufacturing industry. The church of St Valier has an interesting fortified tower and Romanesque doorway. St Girons stands at the very centre of the Pyrenean chain and at the edge of the district of le Comminges. From here a pass leads back towards the main centres of le Comminges over the Portet d'Aspet another of the dramatic passes that leads quickly into the heart of the mountain chain. This area is full of underground caves, the best known being the Juzet d'Izaut Caves which run for thousands of yards through the limestone rock. Here too is the Henne Morte pothole which drops down some fourteen hundred feet into the earth. As the road descends it passes the Pic du Gar over six thousand feet high and a sacred mountain in Roman times.

At the entrance to the village of Fronsac is a keep of the twelfth century, all that remains of a once great castle of the Counts of Comminges. The valley now widens out into a truly prosperous rural scene, with fields full of maize and corn and dotted with bright clean villages.

This is the Valley of Luchon where there is situated the most prosperous town of the whole region. Officially known as Bagnères-de-Luchon it is one of the most popular spas and holiday resorts of the Pyrenees. Set at the foot of the mountain of Superbagnères, while behind is the outline of the grim Port de Venasque, leading across the frontier. It is almost certain that Luchon is the ancient spa of *Thermes Onesiens* of Roman times and its baths and attractions were joined to St Bertrand de Comminges by a special road. The god Ilixo was closely linked with the valley and several sanctuaries were built here in his honour. A substantial amount of the Roman remains so far found have been transported to museums in Toulouse and St Bertrand de Comminges but traces of large baths, marble altars, statues, small baths probably for children and houses have recently been discovered.

All these Roman buildings were destroyed during the Barbarian invasions. During the Middle Ages Luchon suffered from raiding armies of one kind or another and virtually all trace was removed of the spa itself. In 1036 Luchon passed under the House of Aragon but later returned to the Counts of Comminges when that County was reunited with France in 1453. During the War of the Spanish Succession the French under the command of the Marquis de Rozel made a daring attack on the Spanish strongpoint that controlled the Pass of Venasque. The French cleverly hoisted their heavy artillery nearly eight thousand feet up the mountain and used it to force the Spaniards to surrender. Unfortunately the area around Luchon was simultaneously assaulted by the Spaniards who had used another pass and Luchon was again devastated. No sooner had the town recovered in 1723 than a great fire swept through the whole of the built-up area destroying everything except the church.

During the 1750s the Intendant of Auch, a Baron d'Etigny, visited the valley and Luchon, encouraged by chemical analyses of the waters he decided to try to re-open the resort. First he reconstructed the road so that access would be easier and built the fine avenue that now bears his name. This was not greeted with great enthusiasm by the local people, who resented any changes or innovations and for a time troops had to be used to protect these works. D'Etigny then persuaded the Governor of the Province, the Marshal Duc de Richelieu, to come and take a cure. He enjoyed it vastly and recounted his experiences at the French Court, which persuaded in turn the many others to come to try the new found cures. In 1815, a proper thermal establishment was built and from then there has been a continual flow of visitors to the resort. There are some seventy eight different springs in Luchon, all containing differing chemicals, all rather frighteningly radio-active. Its curative powers are reputed to cover such varied illnesses as rheumatism and lung congestion. Many singers come to ease their strained voices.

Some of the finest mountain scenery in the whole of the Pyrenees is reached from Luchon. Just above the town is the small resort of Superbagnères which can be reached either by the funicular railway or by a long winding road. From the top there is a magnificent panorama from the mountain of Crabère in the east to the Arbizon in the west. Just a short distance from Luchon is the famous Hospice de France but the road is narrow and difficult. The Hospice itself is now a hotel set amongst a region of superb mountain walks, wide green slopes, cascading waterfalls and soaring cliffs. From here it is possible to reach the Port de Venasque some eight thousand feet high marking the frontier with Spain.

Gascony reaches its final limits here and to complete our tour of the old province we must turn north once again away from the mountains and down into the great plain of the area fed by the mountain streams. A region rich in agriculture, but above all rich in vines, the vines that produce the very special brandy that has taken its name from this area, the Armagnac.

XIII

CASTLES AND VINES

THE Armagnac is the largest of the old Counties of Gascony and is one of the most diversified. The rivers of the Pyrenees reach out across its plains like wavering blue fingers from the Garonne in the east, to the Save, the Gimone, the Gers, Baïse, the Arros and the Adour in the west. Just north of the Comminges is the Nebouzan, an intermediate area between the mountains and the Haut Armagnac. The Haut Armagnac itself is a region of wide skylines, pleasant rounded slopes with herds of sheep alternating with fields of wheat and corn. Around the town of Auch is the Bas Armagnac which is equally rich in agriculture and cattle. There are relatively few trees in the whole region and no great forests or woods which means that there are vast stretches of grass and crops between the river valleys. Between the Gers and the Arrats is some of the finest countryside of the whole area known as the Fezensaguet with its capital at Vic.

It was around the town of Condom that the vine production was originally based in the limestone soil. Now there are few vineyards here but it is still the centre of the enormous trade in brandy. Originally too, the brandy production was due to the poor quality of the vines of the Gers, and as early as 1752 the Intendant of Etigny said that the wines of the

Gers are too poor in quality to use except in the form of brandy.

The main town of the southern or Bas Armagnac is the local route centre and market town of Auch. One of the most populous places of the whole area, it still has a quaint old town but the most important feature is the cathedral. Originally a settlement of the Iberian tribes, Auch was once known as *Elimberris* the capital of the Ausci people and from whom its later name was to come. The town was sacked in the thirteenth, fifteenth and sixteenth centuries but managed to survive, although losing its place as one time capital of Gascony.

The present town hall is an imposing building of the late eighteenth century with a balcony made out of wrought iron. Nearby is the Museum of Art and Archaeology which is installed in the chapel of the former seminary. Here there is a fine display of South American art. The Tourist Office of Auch has one of the most interesting houses in the town for its offices. It is an attractive fifteenth-century building of brick and wood. Nearby is the Museum of Gascony, where a collection of all the various elements of local life from clothes to furniture, from farming equipment to pottery have been collected. The local services seem to be well installed in Auch for even the library is housed in a former Carmelite Chapel of the seventeenth century. It has a fine collection of books dating back to the thirteenth century including Bibles, Books of Hours and other manuscripts. The local Public Records Office is installed in a former Carmelite Convent and the Prefecture is in what was once the Archbishop's house, a superb construction of the eighteenth century with elaborately decorated pilasters on the façade.

The Cathedral itself, the Ste Marie, is a remarkable building, mostly Gothic with a fine Renaissance façade. It replaced an earlier Gothic building of the thirteenth century which was destroyed by fire in 1483. It stands on the same site as an even earlier Romanesque building. The second rebuilding commenced in 1489 in the flamboyant Gothic style and the Cathedral was consecrated in 1548 but was not completed until the end of the seventeenth century. The interior is grandiose running some three hundred feet long and standing over eighty feet high. The choir stalls are particularly well-carved and are reputed to be the most beautiful of all Renaissance stalls in France. The range of subjects and the inspiration of the carving make the overall effect extremely powerful. There is, in addition, a choir cloister of 1609 built by Pierre Souffron which has an outstanding originality in the use of marble. The choir is also decorated by some stained glass windows, but it is in the chapels that are built around the apse that can be found some of the finest examples, including some painted by Arnaud de Moles in 1513. Each window depicts a scene with characters from both the Old and New Testaments in more than life size. The Mise Au Tombeau with twelve different people in stone in the Chapel of the Trinity is also attributed to de Moles.

Auch forms an excellent point from which to visit this part of Armagnac. Away to the south the road wanders through the pleasant countryside to the town of Saramon, where there are still parts of the old fortified walls. Also of interest is the striking modern church, while two miles away is the Château de St Elix built in 1540. Another modern church is to be found at Castelnau-Barbarens which is built around the old bell tower of the former church. The road soon reaches the rather more important town of Lombez with its old cathedral of Ste Marie brick-built in the fourteenth and fifteenth centuries. It has a forbidding aspect, rather like a fortress. There is a fine eight-sided bell tower and inside the building there are what are considered to be some parts that date from Carolingian times. Shakespeare may at first sight have little to do with this region so far from England and Stratford-upon-Avon but at Samatan the writer Belleforest lived, and it is believed that Shakespeare found inspiration for a number of his great plays from the *Histoires Tragiques* that Belleforest wrote many years before.

Also not far away is the village of Simorre with its perfectly preserved fortified church and the sole remains of a Benedictine Monastery destroyed at the time of the Revolution. Originally built in 1304 it was restored in the fifteenth century and then restored again in 1848 by the famous French architect Viollet-le-Duc, who was appointed by the French Government as head of the Historic Monuments Office. In the nineteenth century the French became increasingly aware of their great architectural heritage and this appointment was a first attempt to preserve this heritage. Viollet-le-Duc is thus best remembered as a restorer. In a few short years he worked on many of the most important buildings of the Middle Ages, in most cases he completed a good job of restoration; however, in some other often less happy cases, he also drastically altered the original with the result that his work, even today, is controversial. Even here he accentuated the military aspect of the church. On the south side there is a fine doorway dating from the thirteenth century. Around the church are some interesting old houses including the old bishop's house, which is now the Post Office.

Another fortified church of some interest can be found at L'Isle-en-Dodon. Built in brick, it dates from the fourteenth century while the eight sided bell-tower dates from the sixteenth century. The inside of the church is well decorated.

A few miles further south is the attractive small town of Carbonne, built on a promontory overlooking the river Garonne. Originally a bastide or small fortified town, built in a regular pattern by the monks of Bonnefont in 1256.

Westward from Auch towards Toulouse the road passes by the valley of the Arcon overlooked by the old Château of St Cricq, the Château of Montegut which dates in part at least from the thirteenth century and a little further on the fine Château du Duc-de-Montesquiou-Fezensac of the eighteenth century. The village of Cahuzac has a charming little chapel built in 1513 and containing some well-carved wooden figures. The ruins of the once powerful and famous Benedictine Abbey of Gimont founded in 1145 lie just above the village. The town of Gimont itself lies a little further on. Built as a bastide in 1265 on a ridge overlooking the river it has a market of the fifteenth or sixteenth century. The church is Gothic and dates from 1506 with a bell tower that was rebuilt in 1704. Inside the church there is a triptyque of the sixteenth century which once belonged to the Abbey of Planselve.

Nearby is the splendid Château de Caumont built in the Renaissance style in 1530 by Pierre de Nogaret La Valette. His grandson the Duc d'Epernon, a favourite of King Henry III was born here. In the rather larger town of L'Isle-Jourdain is the former collegiate church, brick built in 1785 in the classical style. The bell-tower is, in fact, a tower of the original château of the fifteenth century. Here too there is a statue of St Bertrand, first Bishop of Comminges, who was born in the town. In the two main squares are some arcaded walks and covered markets, also a good example of the classic style in the town hall. The very limits of Gascony are reached at Pibrac where behind the church is the Château made again from brick due to the shortage of local building stone. It was built in 1540 by the father of Gui de Faur-de-Pibrac who was the Chancellor of Marguerite de Valois. It has been well restored and has three main buildings with two round towers.

South again from Auch is another town that was once a famous bastide, Mirande. Built in 1285 when it was known as Lezian, it still has parts of its ruined walls which in places have been badly damaged. The church of Notre Dame dates from the fifteenth century and has a large heavy porch. The Museum of Mirande has some good quality paintings and is well worth a visit.

Just a short distance away is the fascinating village of Tillac standing in the valley of the Boues. A picturesque old village, it dates from feudal times. The main street has a series of very old houses held up by wooden columns under their overhanging frontages. There are two defence towers at each end of the village through which the entrance to the village had to be effected. Mielan is another small town, originally founded as a bastide in 1284, on top of a ridge between the valleys of the Osse and the Boues. From the Puntous-de-Laguian there is a famous view out towards the high Pyrenees. The road passes near to St Sever de Rustan with its Romanesque church, and the remains of a Cistercian Abbey, of which the original cloister now stands in the Jardin Massey at Tarbes. Rabastène is another bastide of the early fourteenth century built at the confluence of the Esteoux and the canal Alaric which may have been built by the King of the Visigoths, Alaric, so that there was water for the crops of the valley.

East of Auch the road rises steeply towards the town of Barran which is a bastide built on the usual regular plan. The main gate passes through a fine square tower set in the old fortified walls of which there are substantial remains. There is a charming wooden market hall and an interesting church. The road follows the valley of the river Bäise to L'Isle-de-Noe, a village set between two arms of the river. The town of Montesquiou is a fortified place set on a small hill overlooking the river Osse with its ruined castle of the thirteenth century. It was in this château that the Marshal Montesquiou was born, a son of D'Artagnan.

The road leads on to Bassoues, which is an interesting little village. Just at the entrance to the village are the ruins of a castle once belonging to the Archbishops of Auch and dating from the fourteenth century. The square keep still stands some one hundred and twenty feet high and has three floors within. It is still possible to climb to the top and look out over the vast panorama that the sentinels must have seen in many ways looking very little different from how it looks today. In the village are a number of old houses supported again on wooden piles, while the wooden market hall looks out onto the old castle. In the churchyard is a Basilica of St Fris, which once belonged to the Priory founded in 1020. Badly damaged in the fourteenth and fifteenth centuries it was rebuilt in the nineteenth but of particular interest is that in the large crypt is the burial place of St Fris who was a nephew of Charles Martel, who saved Europe from the Moors at Poitiers. St Fris himself was killed fighting the Moors in a skirmish immediately after the major conflict at Poitiers had been won.

Marciac, is a typical bastide standing on the confluence of the Boues and the Lans. Built in 1298 for the Counts of Pardiac who previously lived in the Château of Monlezun, of which the remains can be seen some miles away. The town has a large main square with fine arcaded walks. The church is built in Gothic style of the fourteenth and fifteenth centuries with a steeple rising to over two hundred feet high.

Turning to the region north of Auch, one of the most important routes runs towards Vic Fezensac through the charming village of Biran. Completely fortified, it overlooks a deep sided valley with its castle keep standing up over all. There is a Romanesque church and a chapel with some interesting stone carvings of the seventeenth century. Vic itself is an important route centre built up on a slope overlooking the river Osse. The church here was built in 1090 and fortified in the fifteenth century, but was later badly damaged during the wars of Religion and restored in 1616. Only the apse remains of the original church but the interior is well decorated. Near to the church are some interesting old houses and other buildings including some fortifications of the fourteenth century. A short distance away is Marambat with its impressive ruined castle and the gates and walls of its old fortifications.

The first town to be the capital of Armagnac was Aignan, now a small quiet village with a church dating from the twelfth century and little else. Manciet lies a little further on with its fine eight-sided bell tower built in the fourteenth century of brick. The next town is Nogaro which owes its foundation to

St Austinde, Archbishop of Auch. Here there is a beautiful church dating from the eleventh century, being substantially Romanesque, of particular interest is the north door which has a tympanum which has been well preserved. Outside the church the cloisters have virtually disappeared, but a small part of the Romanesque still remains.

Aire-sur-l'Adour once known as *Atura* was the seat of Bishops from the year 500 until as recently as 1933 when it was transferred to Dax. The Cathedral fortunately still remains and is, for the most part, as it was when it was built in the twelfth century. It is based on the plan used by the Benedictines for their churches and despite the fact that the apse was rebuilt in the eighteenth century the church as a whole is a fine example of its kind. The town hall now occupies the Bishop's Palace, parts of which date from the twelfth century. Another interesting church is that of the Mas d'Aire sitting on a small hill. It is built of brick and dates from the thirteenth and fourteenth centuries. The beautiful doorway with its tympanum showing the Last Judgement has been damaged but the interior was restored in Classic style leaving six Romanesque arcades in the choir.

The most important town in the Haut Armagnac is Condom. Once a centre full of activity and fine buildings it has now fallen from its high estate but it still keeps its trade in the local Armagnac Brandy. From the time of the Romans the vines of the locality were famous for their products and during the middle ages this cultivation was developed, but mostly in small vineyards. During the Hundred Years War and the Wars of Religion the vines like the people suffered badly, production fell and the large vineyards were left to rot. However, with the return of more peaceful times, the vine-growers prospered and the local wines became well known and appreciated, especially in the time of Napoleon III. By 1873 the region was amongst four or five most important wine producing areas of France. In 1875 the dread disease, which struck so hard at the vine in France, phylloxera, reached the Armagnac with disastrous results and for ten years the work of hundreds of previous years was undone. By the end of the nineteenth century recovery was well under way and with the development of the production of brandy, the vineyards almost rediscovered their old dimensions. It is this growth of the local Armagnac brandy that has done much to maintain the prosperity of the vineyards when products of similar quality in other parts of France have been virtually driven from the market.

Condom still has much of interest to visit, not least the fine town houses of the seventeenth and eighteenth centuries and the old Priory, now a school, with its delightful façade dating from the time of Louis XVI. The most important single building in Condom is the Cathedral of St Pierre, built between 1506 and 1531 by the Bishop Jean Marre. During the Wars of Religion the protestant General Montgomery seized the town, but was dissuaded from destroying the Cathedral by a ransom of thirty thousand livres, a sizeable sum by any standards. Thus it is possible to measure to some extent the value put by people upon their religion and perhaps even more important their religious buildings. The south front has two enormous buttresses while on the west is a heavy square tower. Inside there is some fine vaulting and behind the apse is a chapel of the fourteenth century. Just north of the church is the old Bishops Palace now occupied by the town hall and the law courts. Inside the town hall there is the Musée de l'Armagnac which, although small in size, has some interesting exhibits of local costume and folklore and the development of the Armagnac brandy.

Just north of Condom is the small town of Nérac. Rather like Condom, it has lost the glories of its past and is now a quiet country town. Up until the end of the sixteenth century the town was the court for the Princes of Béarn. Henry of Navarre made his headquarters here whilst he fought what was known as the War of the Lovers in 1580. The town was seized and the defences dismantled by the General Mayenne in 1621 and from then on it lost rapidly in importance. The great Château of Nérac still remains in part but three of the original four wings were destroyed at the time of the Revolution. It is still enough however to give us an idea of the grandeur of the original building surrounding the inner courtyard on all four sides. Across the river are the charming gardens of the Garenne with their own memories of Henry of Navarre for here is the Fountain of Fleurette with a small statue of Fleurette, who was reputed to be a young girl, who worked in the gardens and was seduced by Henry; later when he left her, she drowned herself. The district of Petit Nérac is particularly charming with its old houses some dating from the Middle Ages and others from the Renaissance.

Just on the outskirts of Condom is another interesting small town, La Romieu, which dates from the eleventh century. It grew in riches, both financial and architectural, following the work of Cardinal Arnaud d'Aux who was born here and became Bishop of Albano and who, in 1318, founded the collegiate church and the cloisters, which adjoins it here. The town still has part of the old fortified walls and three gates give access through them.

A little further on, near the town of Astaffort, itself an old fortified town, is the interesting fortified village of Ste Mère. The castle here was built at the end of the thirteenth century by Geraud de Monlezun, Bishop of Lectoure. This castle is a prototype of the so-called *Châteaux Gascons* built in this region at the time of the invasion by the English. Here ran the frontier of the domaine of the English and it was soon heavily fortified. The castles all followed roughly the same design, on a hill overlooking the surrounding countryside. They had no moat or even defensive ditch, being a simple stone keep often square or oblong, with two smaller towers at one end. Access was by a ladder to the first floor level. The ground floor was used as a store, kitchen or armoury and there was no staircase to the upper floors, which also had to be reached by ladders, so strengthening the internal defence. Only a large second floor room was illuminated by windows. Above again was the fortified flat roof with its battlements and watch-towers. Built primarily as strongpoints for the frontier battle some were inhabited as homes, but a rugged and uncomfortable existence it must have been. These castles of Gascony bear a striking similarity to the Pele Towers built on the border of England and Scotland. Belsay Castle, for example, resembles the castle of Herrebouc in Fezensac in virtually every detail. It is evident, however, that these English castles were built in the fourteenth century, while the *Châteaux Gascons* certainly dated from earlier times; perhaps they were the work of some Gascon builders or, at least, were inspired by them.

The town of Lectoure just to the south is another one-time capital of Armagnac. The old cathedral is worth a visit, parts dating back to the twelfth century, it was badly damaged during the Wars of Religion but was extensively restored in the sixteenth century. Near the church is the old Bishop's Palace of the sixteenth and seventeenth centuries, bought by Marshal Lannes, the famous General of Napoleon, who was born here; it was given to the town by his widow. It is now the town hall and contains an interesting lapidary museum full of fine carved stone. Below the Bishops Palace near the old fortified walls is a thirteenth century fountain while on the Cours d'Armagnac are the remains of the Château of the Counts or Armagnac.

To the south is the town of Fleurance, another bastide, built in 1280, it still preserves the same layout, with a charming central square and arcaded walks.

Lying but a short distance to the west of Condom is the unique village of Larresingle, now almost abandoned. It is however one of the finest examples of the original fortified village. Built in the thirteenth century it has a fortified wall enclosing the village proper with a moat to add to its strength. At each corner there is a tower acting as a strongpoint in case of attack. The whole village is dominated by the huge keep of the castle built in 1286 by the Abbot Arnault Othon-de-Lomagne. The castle was the residence of the Bishops of Condom who extended and added to it according to their own particular taste. The church occupies the original ground floor of the keep while the large second floor room was the chapel of the Bishops. The road leads on to another Bastide, that of Montréal. Dating from the thirteenth century it stands on a small hill overlooking the Auzoue river. There are substantial remains of the old fortifications and a church dating from 1300.

Another worth-while visit from Condom is to the Abbaye de Flaran, founded by the Cistercians in the twelfth century. Although damaged by the ever-present Montgomery during his campaigns it is still in an excellent state of preservation. The church dates from the second half of the twelfth century. A fine Romanesque doorway leads from the church to the cloisters which are beautifully laid out. Nearby is the Bastide of Valence-sur-Baïse dating from the thirteenth century, when it was built by the monks of Flaran. It stands on a hill overlooking the confluence of the Baïse and the Auloue. Part of the old walls still remain together with an old castle and a church of the fourteenth century with its façade flanked by two towers.

Castera Verduzan is a small thermal spa, specialising in treating gastric troubles, on the road to Jegun, which stands high above the river Loustère. It has a fine collegiate church with a Romanesque nave.

Easy to reach from Condom is the attractive bastide of Lamontjoie with its Gothic church, which is well decorated. Another bastide near here is at Francescas built as usual on a hill at the end of the thirteenth century. There are some ruins of a castle, that was once occupied by the famous Le Hire one of the Gascon companions in arms of Joan of Arc.

The small town of Eauze stands in a picturesque setting on a steep hill overlooking the Gélise river. Once an ancient Roman city of *Eluza,* the town was destroyed by the Moors in the eighth century but rebuilt two hundred years later. The original Roman town stood on the site of the Château de la Cietat. The church of St Luperc is brick built and dates from around 1500. There are also some interesting old houses, including one on the main square built of wood in the fifteenth century.

We have now come almost full circle for just a short distance away is Mont-de-Marsan and the sandy reaches of the Landes. We have seen much of what has happened in these places in their long and often far from peaceful past, but what of their today. How has this old region faced up to the new problems and challenges of a later era?

XIV
GASCONY TODAY

LIKE many areas that depend on basic agriculture and cattle and sheep raising for a livelihood, Gascony has come but slowly into the twentieth century. Decline in agriculture is a slow process, year by year a few more people leave the land, that no longer produces the crops, that are needed in the great urban and industrial centres, but traditions are so deeply inbred, that these changes are often hardly noticed by the people who live in their midst. But there comes a time when farms have to be grouped into larger units when mechanical aids begin to impinge upon every conscience and the food and crops have to change in type and character to meet new demands.

For the people of Gascony this was a hard transformation, for they are far from these new industries; at least at the start of the twentieth century they were slow to appear. But almost imperceptible at first, change was on the way; and it came first through power. As long as one hundred years ago, progress was being made in harnessing the power of the mountain streams as they gushed and roared down their steep-sided valleys. The first man to attempt this on a large scale was Aristide Berges, who despite the fact that he was born in the Pyrenees made his first experiments in the Dauphiné Alps.

The Pyrenees came but late into the full use of water power some time after the Alps. This was due to a number of factors, not least being the lack of water in the streams during the long and often dry summers. Glaciers, that provided water during the summer in the Alps, are few and far between in the Pyrenees. Another reason was that the region made but little demand from the power, that might have been produced. Eventually however a local engineer, Estrade, set up a power station in the mountains and after the end of the First World War construction commenced to make serious progress in the major valleys of the high Pyrenees, in the valleys of the Aspe and Ossau.

The earlier problems were now being solved and today the vast reservoir of water in the mountain lakes has been used to regulate the flow of the streams throughout the year. To achieve this long tunnels have been driven through some of the highest mountains, to link the different lakes and water sources. In some places remarkable dams at very high levels have been built such as in the valley of the Neste, where the impressive Barrage de Cap de Long holds back a huge lake, which provides an ever growing source of electricity for the national grid.

Yet it was away from the mountains that the second great source of power was found in Gascony. This was the hidden reserves of natural gas and oil which were first found as recently as 1939 at St Marcet near St Gaudens. This led in later years to the most important discovery of oil and natural gas ever made in France which was at Lacq just west of Pau. A vast network of pipeline has been created over the whole region to ensure the smooth distribution of the natural gas. Oil has also been found in commercially usable quantities and quality at Parentis in the Landes, so that France has found at home, a source to supply a large percentage of her petroleum needs.

All these discoveries have had their influence on the Gascons and on Gascony. New industries allied with the new sources of power have appeared. Chemicals and chemical production, light engineering using local electrical power and many allied trades are now established. In addition the needs of the industries have meant building new roads, railways, and airports, so that the new products can be easily and quickly shipped to their customers. In the mountains these changes have been dramatic, roads now run where once not even narrow mule tracks led, and great highways run where once small rocky tracks led up to isolated cols and passes. To build the tunnels through the solid mountain peaks, long cable ways had to be constructed, so that men and materials could reach and work at these dizzy heights.

This has in its turn brought yet another new industry to this region, one which is perhaps not entirely new, but which until recent years was relatively unexploited, that of tourism. Thousands of people can now enjoy the delights of the Landes or the Basque coast, the thrills of the high Pyrenees in the Béarn, the Bigorre or the Comminges. Here too is the perfect area for the real tourist, the man who wishes to tour whether it be by car, by bicycle or on foot wherever the charm of the countryside and the history of the Armagnac is to be explored.

Gascony has not been slow to develop its tourist attractions. As we have seen, the whole region, but in particular the mountain region, has been famous since the days of the Romans for its thermal waters. These are waters that are forced out of the earth's surface at some weak spot, usually on the line of some ancient volcanic activity; very often the waters are hot and always rich in chemicals, for they have been forced through great depths under considerable pressure. The curative powers of these waters have been known and used for the treatment of disease, illness and injury for thousands of years.

But it was only in the eighteenth century that they began to develop, when they attracted the rich clientèle of those rather expansive days. Although for a time they fell out of fashion, the spas of the Pyrenees are now once again fully patronised, mostly by the French themselves, and as it is sometimes claimed, thanks to the French health service aiding in the financing of taking a cure. Many spas, realising that nowadays offering its water to the sick and elderly is not enough, have developed as holiday resorts, offering excursions into the mountains, sports and games such as tennis or golf, and many now have delightful and usually well-heated swimming pools.

Thanks to their situation these spas make excellent centres for walking holidays with walks of varying difficulty from a stiff mountain climb to a quiet afternoon stroll. Many of the most interesting routes have been marked, so that the keen walker can cover considerable distances through the magnificent mountain scenery. It is common enough to find walkers far up in the high peaks and valleys tramping happily along, usually with their own camping equipment, map and compass. One word of warning for intending walkers or climbers or even just holiday makers; it is advisable never to go into the mountains without adequate clothing and this means warm waterproof outer clothes and strong waterproof shoes or boots. It is only when one spends a few days in the mountains that one can appreciate how quickly the lovely sunny morning can change into the miserable cold misty afternoon.

It is in the mountains too that some of these resorts have found a new vocation in the winter months. Where once all the hotels and tourist facilities closed down as soon as the last summer visitor left, now a new season begins. This is the vast and rapid expansion of winter sports. Once again the Pyrenees were rather slower in development than the Alps, but now cable cars and ski lifts seem to run up every mountain. The roads and passes once blocked by snow for months on end are open to traffic and skiers and skaters slide and cavort on snow and ice, which once meant nothing more to the peasant farmer than a long period of hardship to be borne as well as possible every winter. Now this growth of popularity of winter sports has reached such a stage that the facilities of the older resorts are no longer enough and entirely new towns, designed to cope with the winter holidaymaker, are being built. Bright modern villages with smart wood and plastic hotels and shops abound, while the skiers themselves seem to match the shops and houses with the brightness of the colours of their attire. It is strange, almost incongruous, to come upon one of these *stations de ski* in this old countryside, often nearby or even part of some old village with a history going back to Roman times.

But it is perhaps in summer that Gascony has most to offer the visitor. This, as we have seen, is a great region for the tourist who travels with his motor car. Here are those pleasant country inns, for which France is so famous; a simple room and a meal to remember for the cost of but a few shillings is the reward of those who take the trouble to wander just a little away from the terrifying main roads, that carry their streams of hurrying people through Gascony and on to Spain or Portugal or even further.

From some pleasant country town in the Armagnac the whole historic region can be reached and explored and enjoyed with remarkable ease. Never far from the sea and the wide clean sandy beaches, every holiday need seems to be met. Motoring in the mountains themselves is only slightly more difficult, but the carefully graded roads, the steady climbs up the weaving hairpin bends make even the most apparently terrifying col seem like just another drive. Before setting off on mountain driving, it is as well to spend some time to ensure that the basic essentials of your car work, in particular brakes and cooling system; it is worth remembering that the higher you go the less efficient your engine will become, so some loss of performance is to be expected.

Even the guards of the National Park in their hardy Land

Rovers pay more than average attention to these points. But the mountains hold many delights for the simple motorist, once the techniques of the steep climb and the sharp turn have been learnt, the superb views and the thrills of the mountain are yours to enjoy. Accommodation and food although often unpretentious are worth many a long detour. Fresh-caught trout or the local *Garbure,* a sort of cabbage and bacon soup made thick with seasonable vegetables is enough to satisfy the hungriest traveller. Today, many motorists carry their own accommodation with them in the form of tent or caravan, although following a car towing a large caravan over the Col D'Aubisque can be a frightening experience, in fact it is quite safe and thousands pass in security every year. Gascony, like many other areas of France is well-equipped with first class camping sites, which in some ways are just like hotels with restaurant, showers, games-rooms and even swimming pools.

The motor-car does have one serious disadvantage and this is that it makes distance a relative thing; how much more satisfactory it is to get out of your car and walk through the mountains themselves gathering lasting memories and impressions at every step. On the plains too there is the same problem for the roads in France permit far greater speed than most in Britain and in the dash to get from one place to another, how many charming villages, historic castles or quiet churches are left in a rush with hardly a passing glance. In this way the true aspects of each region are often missed, but in Gascony what should never be missed are the local specialities, the *pâté de foie gras* of the Landes has a delicacy all of its own, even if the goose is cruelly stuffed with maize to fatten it all the more quickly. It is a region famous for its preserves; these comprise the best parts of the goose and of the duck stored in its own fat, to be eaten in the long winter months. The Basques as becomes them, have some dishes all of their own including the excellent *piperade*, a mixture of egg, tomatoes and peppers and the rather more solid *Gâteau Basque*. There is, of course, the popular Bayonne ham made and eaten far and wide in the whole region. It is claimed that the isard, the local mountain goat or chamois, makes good eating, but there are so few and these are so well protected that it is now virtually impossible to find one to cook.

For many years the natural life of the region and particullarly the animals that lived in the mountains suffered depredations from hunters, other animals such as wild dogs and predators, to such an extent that some of the most important

species including the graceful and agile isards were in danger of disappearing. Wolves had already been eliminated and the great pride of the mountains the Pyrenean bear was becoming more and more rare. With the growing flood of tourists and the ever-improving means of access to the once never disturbed high slopes time had come to find a solution. This problem was resolved by the setting up of a National Park for the Pyrenees. The official objects of the National Park are threefold, first to protect, for the benefit of science and future generations, the flora and fauna as well as the natural conditions under which they live. Secondly to ensure that in our urban and industrial society there is somewhere for people to go where they can find nature undisturbed. Thirdly to maintain the old pattern of rural life, particularly where due to the marginal character of its economy it is in danger of disappearing.

In the Pyrenees the park covers the frontier area in the departments of the Hautes and Basses Pyrenees for some seventy miles and it has a depth that varies from a maximum of ten miles to a minimum of one mile. The altitude varies from three thousand three hundred feet to over ten thousand feet at the peak of Vignemale. The whole area is empty of any permanent population except for the occasional shepherd or cattleherd. It covers some of the most dramatic mountain scenery in the whole of France, including the high mountains, forests, glaciers and more than one hundred lakes and streams. The total area is some one hundred thousand acres. The park is under the direction of a special board, mostly local people, but the day to day running is carried out by a director assisted by two technical assistants and thirty five guards or wardens. The French Ministry of Agriculture has overall responsibility. A great deal of work has been completed since the park was set up in 1967. Many miles of footpaths have been marked and laid out, refuge huts have been built or renovated, car parks, information centres and map boards have been established. In addition to the park itself there is what is known as a peripheral zone, which covers the area adjacent to the park. This is where visitors can come and stay in hotels or camping sites and where the local tourist industry, local agriculture and the local arts receive special encouragement from the authorities.

Inside the park itself the rules laid down to protect the animals and plants are reduced to the minimum; in brief all hunting is banned absolutely, neither may any animal no matter how small be trapped, injured or carried off. Animals must not be disturbed particularly in their nest or homes, and no other foreign animals such as dogs may be brought into the park. Fishing, however, is allowed for a large programme of development of the fish of the mountain lakes has brought the population of such fish as trout up to acceptable levels. Plants, too, are completely protected and must not be touched, cut or dug up. In this way, it is hoped that certain plants that have become very rare may have the chance to grow and flourish.

Happily the Spaniards have created a park on their side of the frontier which covers virtually the same boundaries as the French park. In addition they have the National Park of Ordesa which has been in existence for many years. The park lies immediately behind the Cirque de Gavarnie and is now very rich in animal life.

But what of the animals themselves, what can actually be seen in the Park? The largest of all the animals is the Pyrenean Brown Bear, but it is very rarely seen by anyone let alone visitors in the Park. Very few bears remain, perhaps thirty or forty at most, and this is really a guess based on observation of the occasional footprint, a tree slashed by a bear sharpening its claws, the remains of a sheep eaten by the bears or, even more rarely, the dead body of a bear found. The bear itself stands over six feet high and weighs nearly four hundred pounds when fully grown, so that one would think that it would not be difficult to see, even in the densest forest. But the bear is very cautious hardly ever coming out during the day and keeping far away from man. Bears live on fruit, roots, insects, snails, rats, and frogs and, very rarely, on sheep or a pig, so that they do not need to hunt near to haunts of man. For the most part then they live in the deepest most inaccessible parts of the forests, above the valleys of the Aspe and Ossau.

As we have seen, the most common animal is the isard. For some years the isard had been protected in two small nature reserves at Ossau and the Neouville. Now there are already some one thousand five hundred isards in the park and their numbers are constantly increasing. They are also becoming less timid, but will still keep a respectable distance away up on their rocky crags. Another interesting animal, that had at one time completely disappeared, is the marmot. Recently re-introduced, they can be seen with the help of field glasses jumping and cavorting around their rocky homes whistling shrilly one to another.

Amongst the birds some of the most common are the partridge and the Coq de Bruyère, which is similar to the grouse. More impressive are the great vultures who swing idly above the mountain peaks seeking out some sheep fallen from high rock or ledge. Each vulture seems to have its own territory to patrol and, as soon as it sights some likely food source it descends slowly towards it, followed by the vultures from neighbouring areas; soon vultures have appeared from miles away and any carcass is soon stripped. With their nine feet wingspan, they make an exceptionally fine sight, as they circle and hover in the clear air. Very rare now are the golden eagles, which once were known from one end to the other of the Pyrenees.

More common are the black and yellow salamanders. There are also snakes, including numbers of vipers. Also interesting are the lizards which vary greatly in size from the usual small grey lizards to the large green lizard which may, it is said, grow to great size in its body being as thick as the forearm of a man. There are many types of frogs living in the swampy ground near the Gaves. There is an entirely different form of life in the many caves and grottoes both inside and outside the national park. Here one can find bats, mice and many strange and wonderful insects. One cannot leave the animals of the Pyrenees without mentioning the famous Pyrenean Mountain dog, now, regrettably few in number. An old race of dogs, it is certainly older than the St Bernard or even the Labrador. These dogs are large indeed with thick white fur to resist the mountain cold. The true sheepdog, in the words of one writer, 'he did not look after the sheep, he protected them against bears, wolves or thieves. Faithful and resourceful he would stay on guard all night without relief or encouragement'.

So the Pyrenees have taken steps to protect its heritage of natural life in a region that is now safe from the depredations of man. Here then are the mountains as they were and as they will be. Change may come to the lower valleys, to the old farms, to the people whether they be Basque or Gascons, but it is in the bare rocky high places that things do not change. As they looked down on the Iberians, the Romans, the Barbarians, the Moors, the Spaniards, the Black Prince, the French, Wellington, those who fled from the terrors of the Spanish Civil War and those who fled from Hitler's Europe to join the Allied forces, so the mountains still look down today over the plain and out towards the Atlantic.

INDEX

A

B

G

H

I

J

L